LANGUAGE *in*ACTION

A GUIDE TO COMPREHENDING AND COMPOSING

Leaving Certificate English *Ordinary Level*

JOHN SHEIL

Published by
C J Fallon
Ground Floor – Block B
Liffey Valley Office Campus
Dublin 22

First edition March 2009

© John Sheil

Acknowledgements

The publishers and author gratefully acknowledge the following for permission to reproduce copyright material: Random House Group Ltd for extracts from *The Curious Incident of the Dog in the Night-time* by Mark Haddon and *The Boy in the Striped Pyjamas* by John Boyne; HarperCollins Publishers for extracts from *Wild Swans* by Jung Chang, *The Things they Carried* by Tim O'Brien and *Girl with a Pearl Earring* by Tracy Chevalier; Bloomsbury Ltd for an extract from *The Kite Runner* by Khaled Hosseini; Penguin Group (USA) for an extract from *The Secret Life of Bees* by Sue Kidd; Penguin Group (UK) for an extract from *About a Boy* by Nick Hornby; Jonathan Williams Literary Agency for an extract from *The Gift of the Gag* (edited by Stephen Dixon and Deirdre Falvey); PFD London for 'The Lesson in the Classroom' by Roger McGough; *Irish Independent*; *Sunday Times*; *Irish Times*; Show Racism the Red Card Campaign; Irish Cancer Society; Office of the European Council.

Every effort has been made to secure permission to reproduce copyright material in this book. However, if the publishers have inadvertently overlooked any copyright holders, they will be pleased to come to a suitable arrangement with them at the earliest opportunity.

Printed in Ireland by
Kilkenny People Printing
Purcellsinch
Carlow Road
Kilkenny

CONTENTS

INTRODUCTION

The aim of this book is to help Ordinary Level students to develop the language and thinking skills that are needed in order to become effective users of language.

The central focus is on **Comprehending** and **Composing**, the two areas tested in Paper 1 of the Leaving Certificate English examination.

In **Section I** (Comprehending) of Paper 1, the student is given texts to read and is then expected to answer related questions. In **Section II** (Composing), the student must write on one of a choice of compositions.

In total, the paper accounts for 200 marks, divided in the following way:

- **Comprehending – 100 marks**

  Question A – 50 marks

  Question B – 50 marks

- **Composing – 100 marks**

COMPREHENDING

Section I presents you with texts to read and can take either a visual or written format. Types of text include the following:

- Diary
- Report
- Letter
- Advertisement
- Novel
- Speech
- Articles
- Visuals

Obviously, when longer texts – such as novels and speeches – are examined, only extracts are used in the examination paper.

There are two parts in Section I – **Question A** and **Question B**.

Question A

This section asks you to examine a number of texts. You must read these carefully and answer questions on the material. For example, you will be asked about the content, purpose and style of the texts.

Question B

These are functional writing exercises. You might be asked to write a letter, a short report, an article or speech based on your reading of the texts.

COMPOSING

These are longer writing exercises and include a personal account, short story, article and speech.

All texts have:

- An author
- A purpose
- Content (i.e. something to say)
- An audience

Always ask:

- **Who** is the writer? (author)
- **Why** is it written? (purpose)
- **What** is it about? (content)
- For **whom** is it written? (audience)

In addition, the candidate should ask:

- **How** is it written? (style)

IMPORTANT TERMS

The following key terms should be studied carefully and understood before approaching Paper 1.

- **TEXT** – Anything in a written or visual form. Examples: novels, articles, letters, photographs. Each comprehension passage in your exam is a text.
- **AUTHOR** – Anybody who writes a text, e.g. songwriter, novelist, journalist, copywriter, diarist, speech writer, poet, etc.

- **PURPOSE** – The reason for which a text is written. It can be to inform, entertain, explain, persuade, teach, convince, etc.

- **CONTENT** – What a text is about. The subject of the text, e.g. a match report will give details about the game.

- **AUDIENCE** – Those for whom a text is written. This can be a very large or a small group of readers. For example, the Harry Potter books, an advertisement for mortgages, horror films, text messages, all have different audiences.

- **STYLE** – This is the way a text is written. A writer's style depends upon audience, purpose, content. Consider how you use language to text, to apply for jobs, to write a story.

- **LAYOUT** – Letters, reports, reviews, and poems are presented in different ways. Layout includes headings, paragraphs, visuals, bullet points, etc.

SOME NOTES ON LANGUAGE

FORMAL

This is the type of language that is used in business, when being polite, or in situations when you do not know the person very well. The following sentences are examples of formal speech and writing:

- "I am writing to complain about the service that I received at your store on Tuesday last."

- "Gathered guests, I want to thank you all for attending this very happy event."

- "Before using this appliance, ensure that you read the instructions carefully."

INFORMAL

This is the type of language that is used with friends or with people with whom we are relaxed. Examples of informal language include the following sentences:

- "Listen up, I'm starting a new chapter and the beginning is very important."

- "I hope you are feeling better after the party last weekend."

- "Thanks for showing up; it's really great to see you all again after so many years."

COLLOQUIAL

This type of language is even more relaxed. It is the language of everyday speech and the words are often shortened. The following sentences are examples:

- "Hiya, haven't seen you in yonks!"

- "The gig was great. There were, like, loads of me mates there."

- "The girls were dolled up and looking amazing...the lads were, well, just looking."

DESCRIPTION

Language that paints a picture is called descriptive language. This uses:

- Verbs
- Adjectives
- Adverbs
- Similes
- Metaphors
- Personification

Example

The cars crawled towards the airport. Like a multi-coloured snake, the line of traffic wound round the city. In the bus lanes, yellow taxis whizzed past, bringing their passengers to busy terminals. A heavy hammer was pounding in Jake's head. He was worried about being late. "Nobody is going anywhere without me," he joked to himself. Today, he would be starting his new job as the pilot on flight WH46, bound for Manchester.

TONE

Tone is the author's (or writer's) attitude to the subject. Can you identify the tone of each of the following? (*Hint*: bitter, angry, sarcastic, joyful)

- "For the last time, stop making that noise!"
- "If only you had helped me when I was down, I wouldn't now be in this mess."
- "We returned from holidays with great memories, and photographs of new friends and presents for loved ones."
- "Don't bother helping. I can obviously manage very well on my own."

Questions

For each of the following, state (a) the audience, and (b) whether the language will be formal or informal:

1. Job application letter.
2. Diary entry.
3. Letter to the editor of a broadsheet newspaper.
4. Speech to your classmates.
5. Party political broadcast on national television.
6. Best man's wedding speech.
7. Stand-up comedian's routine.
8. Sermon in church.

PART I

COMPREHENSION

This section of the book focuses on comprehending. For the Leaving Certificate examinations, you will be asked to attempt two kinds of comprehending tasks. These are dealt with in separate chapters.

Question A

This consists of reading a text (or visual) and answering three or four fairly short questions.

Question B

A functional writing exercise. You may be asked to write a letter, a speech, an article, a report or some other kind of functional task.

CHAPTER 1

COMPREHENDING
QUESTION A

Question A of Section I is worth 50 marks in the examination. You are required to read and answer questions on a text. A choice of texts is given and you have to answer three questions on the text that you pick. In the examination, you will meet both written and visual texts.

This chapter will provide examples of a variety of texts and will offer help on answering questions.

REMEMBER

- Read the question carefully.
- Read the comprehension text.
- Underline what you need for your answer.
- Write out your answer.
- Keep your answers focused and reasonably short.

Three points are normally sufficient. Support your answer using short quotations from, and references to, the passage.

The questions are usually on the following areas:

- The content.
- The language and style.
- Your reaction to the text.

Examining Texts

Examine the three texts that follow. Keep your focus on the following aspects:

| Author | Purpose | Content | Audience | Style | Layout

❦ T E X T 1 ❧

BEND IT LIKE BECKHAM

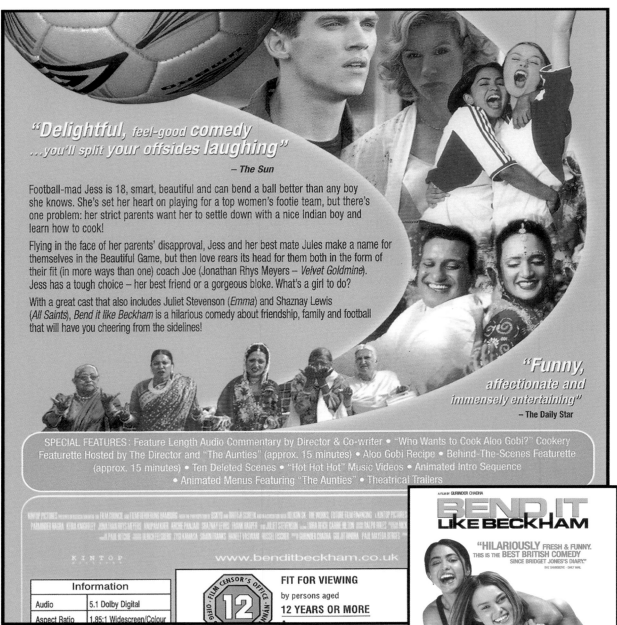

*"Delightful, feel-good comedy
...you'll split your offsides laughing"*
– The Sun

Football-mad Jess is 18, smart, beautiful and can bend a ball better than any boy
she knows. She's set her heart on playing for a top women's footie team, but there's
one problem: her strict parents want her to settle down with a nice Indian boy and
learn how to cook!

Flying in the face of her parents' disapproval, Jess and her best mate Jules make a name for
themselves in the Beautiful Game, but then love rears its head for them both in the form of
their fit (in more ways than one) coach Joe (Jonathan Rhys Meyers – *Velvet Goldmine*).
Jess has a tough choice – her best friend or a gorgeous bloke. What's a girl to do?

With a great cast that also includes Juliet Stevenson (*Emma*) and Shaznay Lewis
(*All Saints*), *Bend it like Beckham* is a hilarious comedy about friendship, family and football
that will have you cheering from the sidelines!

*"Funny,
affectionate and
immensely entertaining"*
– The Daily Star

SPECIAL FEATURES : Feature Length Audio Commentary by Director & Co-writer • "Who Wants to Cook Aloo Gobi?" Cookery
Featurette Hosted by The Director and "The Aunties" (approx. 15 minutes) • Aloo Gobi Recipe • Behind-The-Scenes Featurette
(approx. 15 minutes) • Ten Deleted Scenes • "Hot Hot Hot" Music Videos • Animated Intro Sequence
• Animated Menus Featuring "The Aunties" • Theatrical Trailers

www.benditbeckham.co.uk

Information	
Audio	5.1 Dolby Digital
Aspect Ratio	1.85:1 Widescreen/Colour

FIT FOR VIEWING
by persons aged
12 YEARS OR MORE

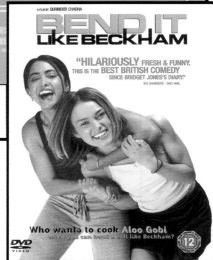

Comprehending

1. What is the purpose of this text?

2. What do we learn about the film?

3. To whom might this film appeal?

4. Identify three colloquial words or phrases in this text?
   Why is this language used?

5. Do you think the visual image has been well chosen?

6. In what way is the DVD made appealing? Examine both the visual and the
   written elements.

✍ TEXT 2 ✍

This extract is from Pete McCarthy's travel book McCarthy's Bar. *The book is an account of a journey he made around Ireland. In this extract, he visits Dingle, Co. Kerry.*

Some time in 1984, a young dolphin began to appear in Dingle Harbour. Unusually for such sociable mammals, he was always alone. He started visiting every day and was soon christened Fungi. Word was out among the New Age and hippy communities, who came down to bond with him. It wasn't long before he was marketed to the mainstream, and a raft of Fungie-related cottage industries grew up around him – boat trips and swimming sessions and wet-suit hire and books and photos and hostels. Suddenly Dingle was no longer remote. It had become a Destination, recommended by all the *Rough* and *Lonely Planet Guides*, with a marketing strategy, and an increasing sense of organised craic.

When you think about it, it's remarkable how reliable Fungie has been, turning up on cue every day for fifteen years for people to photograph and swim with him. For a wild dolphin, that is exceptional behaviour, and also very good for business. I can't quite banish the lingering suspicion that there's a guy who dresses up in the dolphin suit every day. The bottom will fall out of the tourist boom once he decides he's too knackered to do it any more. If they've any sense, they'll already be training up a replacement. There was a Dutch guy with very muscular arms in De Valera's Bar this morning, who wanted to know if he could have fish for breakfast. Maybe it's him.

Comprehending ▮

1. According to the extract, what draws people to Dingle?

2. What is the purpose of this extract?

3. Did you find this a humorous piece of writing? Give reasons for your answer.

4. Who do you think might be the audience for this book?

5. How would you describe the author's tone (serious or humorous) in this extract? You must give reasons for your answer.

∞ T E X T 3 ∞

SAO MIGUEL

This extract is taken from a holiday brochure issued by Sunway Travel

Sao Miguel

From the vibrancy of the city life with its museums and palaces of art and historical treasures, to the tranquillity of lush green countryside punctuated by colourful flowers and volcanic lakes, Sao Miguel makes the perfect holiday destination.

Whether you like golf, tennis, walking, cycling, deep sea diving or are keen to go horse riding, sailing or whale watching or simply relax on the beach by day and enjoy gourmet cuisine by night, this unique island provides activities for the whole family.

Places of Interest

• The Sant'Ana' Palace, a 19th century construction surrounded by beautiful gardens.

• The museum Carlos Machado in Ponta Delgada, an excellent institution with permanent exhibitions.

• The Lagoa do Fogo (Fire Lake). Hikers may reach the lake by well travelled paths.

• The Furnas Lake, surrounded by a beautiful flowered shore.

Please Note: For all two centre and island visits, transfer rates have not been included in the price panels as we recommend car hire for clients to explore the island. Please call our reservations team to book your car hire for your island tours.

Comprehending

1. What is the purpose of this text?

2. Look at the writing and the visual. To whom might this destination appeal?

3. What do you like or not like about the way this has been presented?

4. What attractions does the resort offer to tourists?

THE PURPOSES OF TEXTS

In the Leaving Certificate, you will encounter texts that use language for the purposes of:

- Information
- Persuasion/Argument
- Narration

Note: Texts can often have more than one purpose. Consequently, you will find texts that inform and persuade, or tell a story and give information.

TEXTS THAT GIVE INFORMATION

- You must be able to identify the information that the text gives to its audience.
- You must be able to say how the information is given.

Information can be educational, useful, entertaining, for our safety, and so on.

Common features of informative writing include:

- Use of facts and statistics.
- Written in a clear style.

Examples: newspaper reports, manuals, guides, biographies, etc.

Texts 4 and 5 are examples of texts that provide information. Read them carefully and answer the questions that follow.

⸰❧ T E X T 4 ❧⸰

BIG IS BEAUTIFUL

This is a newspaper article that was written to give information about the world's biggest ship, the Freedom.

The *Freedom* is the most eagerly awaited cruise ship in history.

Surfing on deck; water volleyball in a dedicated sports pool; ice-skating in the Caribbean; you can do all this – and much more – on the 158,000 ton giant that cost almost €700 million. It's owned by Royal Caribbean International.

Crowds turned up in Southampton to look enviously on as a fireworks display lit up the night sky in advance of *Freedom's* departure for New York. For the sporty, the Flow Rider instructors teach holidaymakers the ups (and many downs) of surfing. For families, the Kids Club area is enormous, with online gaming, treasure hunts, art classes and so on. The teenagers are also supervised by the ship's staff and can while away their time with a huge arcade games area and night time disco.

For the less energetic, the ship's main focal point is an enormous Royal Promenade, boasting an English-style pub, an American-style wine bar, Champagne Bar, barber's shop, gift and fashion stores and duty-free shop. At the end is the Arcadia Theatre, which would dwarf many venues in Ireland, where nightly Broadway and Vegas style entertainment is put on to keep the guests happy.

For our dinner (black tie and cocktail dresses, of course), there was a mouth-watering variety of cuisines.

After dinner, we checked out the casino (a mini-Vegas, straight out of *Oceans Eleven*), quaffed champers in the Schooner Bar, while listening to Latino sounds, and danced the night away in the huge Crypt nightclub. And if that's enough to give you the munchies, you can pick up the phone and get food direct to your room 24/7. The only hard part was disembarking the next morning into the English drizzle.

Comprehending

1. The ship is described as a 'giant'. What facts about the ship in the article make this seem an accurate description?

2.   Are you impressed by this ship? Give reasons for your answer.

3.   What kind of person would go on a cruise aboard the *Freedom*? Support your answer with references to the text.

⊷ T E X T 5 ⊷

WHAT IS THE INTERNET?

This extract is taken from a book called Everything You Pretend To Know and Are Afraid Someone Will Ask *by Lynette Padwa.*

The Internet is a huge international computer network made up of other computer networks. It is changing and growing every day, as new networks and users plug into it. The Internet is an important part of the information superhighway.

The Net, as it's called, began in 1969 as a U.S. government experiment. The goal was to enable academic and military researchers around the country and the world to communicate with one another. It was designed to keep working in the event of nuclear attack. That meant the system had to be decentralised, so that there was no Internet 'headquarters' that could be bombed, thus disabling the system.

The Internet has expanded enormously in 25 years and has become easily accessible. The upside is that the Net provides an extraordinary free 'town square' where people can exchange ideas, look for information, buy and sell, download music and films, etc. One of the downsides is that the Net can be very intimidating to newcomers and can spread harmful information. The numbers and the rate of growth are mind-boggling. In 1992, there were 727,000 Internet-registered computers; in 1994, there were 25 million.

There are now 1,407,724,920 people on-line.

The size of the Net shouldn't in itself be daunting – after all, the fact that there are millions of cars on the road doesn't prevent people from driving. The problem has been gaining access to the Net and, once you are on it, finding your way around. Getting on the Internet has become much easier in recent years.

Now you can get on the Internet by signing on with a choice of service providers. You can also plug into it directly as long as your computer is equipped to do so.

Comprehending

1. How did the Internet begin?

2. Write down two advantages and two disadvantages of the Internet. Use the information in this extract in your answer.

3. Write a short article (similar to the article above) called 'What is Texting?'

TEXTS THAT USE PERSUASION AND ARGUMENT

When dealing with texts that use persuasion and argument, the following should be considered:

- You must be able to say what the audience is being persuaded to accept.
- You must be able to say how the text persuades its audience.

Features of persuasive language include:

- An appeal to our feelings and emotions – use of strong positive or negative words.
- An appeal to our sense of what is right and wrong.
- An appeal to our reason – by using examples.

Examples of texts that use persuasion include advertisements, letters to the newspaper, editorials, articles, speeches, etc.

The texts that follow – Text 6 to Text 9 – are examples of different types of persuasive texts.

❧ TEXT 6 ❧

GOVERNMENT HEALTH WARNINGS

Smoking Kills

Smoking seriously harms you and others around you

Smoking when pregnant harms your baby

Comprehending I

1.   What is the purpose of these statements?

2.   Who is the intended audience for these warnings?

3.   In what ways is the language used persuasively?

4.   Do you think these warnings are effective?

∽ T E X T   7 ∾

ADVICE LEAFLET

This leaflet was produced by the Irish Cancer Society. Examine it carefully.

THE
MAKE-UP OF
SMOKING

After cleansing, exfoliating, toning and moisturising, how about some poisoning?

Considering the care with which you choose your face creams, perhaps you should consider this: every cigarette contains 4,000 toxins, many of which your blood stream carries right into the structure of your skin. So how do you cleanse there?

201 203 • call the quitline: 1850 201 203 •

BREAK FREE
TAKE CONTROL
OF YOUR LIFE

ALL THE HELP YOU NEED...

If you'd like some advice on quitting, you can call the National Quitline on callsave 1850 201 203

You can also talk to your GP or Pharmacist or the Local Health Board

And whatever you do, always remember that you are not alone : 70% of smokers want to quit! Good luck. You can do it.

For further information call the Irish Cancer Society Health Promotion Department on 01 231 0500

irish cancer society

THE BEAUTY OF QUITTING

DEAR QUITLINE

I'm 29 and I smoke. I understand all the logical reasons why I should quit, but I just can't seem to do it. I know the Why, but I don't know the How. Got any advice?   SMOKER

Dear Smoker,

We are delighted that you are thinking of quitting - here are our TOP 10 TIPS

1. Prepare Yourself
Write down your reasons for stopping and keep them close at hand.

2. Set a Date
Get rid of all cigarettes - light/low tar cigarettes are not an option and are just as bad.

3. Ask for Help
Get some support from your family and friends.

4. Watch out for Triggers
Break your routine for a while by avoiding the things you normally associate with smoking, e.g. coffee and alcohol.

5. Get some Exercise
Exercise helps reduce stress and keeps you fit.

6. Reward Yourself
Open a separate account and, once a month, put away what you'd normally spend on tobacco. Then, treat yourself with the money you have saved.

7. Learn to Cope with Cravings
Cravings are normal and may be part of your life for a while.

4 D's to deal with Cravings:
• Delay at least 3 minutes and the urge will pass;
• Drink a glass of water or fruit juice;
• Distract yourself;
• Deep breathe slowly and relax.

8. Think Positive
Withdrawal symptoms that may occur are temporary. Keep feeling good about yourself.

9. Watch what you Eat
Avoid snack attacks with things like chocolate or biscuits. Try fruit or some sugar-free gum instead.

10. Take One Day at a Time
Every day without cigarettes is good news for your health, your family and your pocket.

itline: 1850 201 203 • call the quitline: 185(

LOOK GREAT FEEL FREE

WHEN YOU QUIT....

• You'll be free from the dependence on nicotine

• You'll be free to enjoy an active, energetic life

• You'll be free from the worry that you're damaging your health, as well as that of your family and friends

• You'll significantly reduce your risk of heart disease and smoking related cancers

• You'll be free from the effects of 4,000 chemicals, including tar and carbon monoxide

• You'll be free from the financial burden of cigarettes

SO HOW CAN SMOKING AFFECT ME?

- Smokers lose an average of 10 -15 years of potential life.
- Smoking causes 90% of lung cancers in women. Smoking also greatly increases your risk of getting many other cancers, including cancer of the cervix.
- Smoking is a major risk factor for heart disease and causes bronchitis and emphysema.
- If you're a smoker and you're taking the contraceptive pill, you increase your risk of heart attack and stroke.
- If you're planning on having a baby, remember that smoking can reduce your fertility and that smoking during pregnancy can lead to miscarriage, stillbirth and illness in early infancy.
- If you smoke, you're likely to reach menopause 2 - 3 years earlier.

GOOD LOOKS

Some people think smoking looks sophisticated. But looks can be deceptive.

In fact, smokers' skin wrinkles and ages prematurely.

And puckering your lips when you inhale gives you wrinkles around your mouth.

Not to mention discoloured fingernails, yellowing of teeth and bad breath.

The longer you don't smoke, the longer you'll keep your good looks.

201 203 • call the quitline: 1850 201 203 • call the quitline: 1850 201 203 • call the quit

Comprehending

1. At what groups of people in our society is this leaflet is aimed? Refer to the leaflet in your answer.

2. Explain why a reader might be persuaded to give up smoking after reading this article. Give three reasons.

3. Do you think that this is a well produced leaflet? Refer in your answer to the layout, use of colour and illustrations.

ꕢ T E X T   8 ꕢ

EDITORIAL

The editor of a newspaper often gives the newspaper's opinion on topical issues. In the following editorial from the Irish Times, *the subject of fireworks at Halloween is addressed.*

Every year around this time, the elderly in particular and others of a nervous disposition are forced to take cover in their homes as blasts from illegal fireworks shatter the quiet of afternoons and evenings and often continue long into the night. Further distress is caused by the suffering inflicted on domestic pets, especially dogs.

When used inappropriately, fireworks have the potential to inflict life-changing injuries. Each year, many people lose fingers, damage or lose eyes and suffer other such horrific accidents. Food for thought this weekend.

Comprehending

1. What is the purpose of this editorial?
2. According to this editorial, what problems do fireworks cause at Halloween?
3. Do you think that the author makes his or her point in a fair way?

ꕢ T E X T   9 ꕢ

TEENS AND SMOKING

In this newspaper article, the subject of teenage smoking is addressed.

No parent, not even an inveterate smoker, wants to see their child with a cigarette. The warnings that fill us with fear, however, **cause teens to tune out faster than** a panel discussion on government taxation policy.

The fear of possibly getting lung cancer or heart disease somewhere in the distant future only interests a child until the next time someone offers them a cigarette. At this point, they simply get on with the business of fitting in.

The present generation is more switched on to global issues than any that went before. For parents who are looking for some useful arguments for young people to use in their personal battle with cigarettes and as a justification to their friends, here are some non-health-related disadvantages to smoking.

◆ The tobacco industry is one of the biggest employers of children in the world. Child labour is thought to account for up to one third of all tobacco output.

◆ Tobacco companies work hardest selling to countries where poverty and war have made it difficult for governments to inform their own people of the dangers of smoking. Cigarette smoking is on the rise in countries where the health of the population is already weakened by poverty and disease.

◆ In poor regions, such as Eastern Europe, South America and Africa, tobacco companies give away free cigarettes to children to encourage addiction.

◆ If cigarettes are not meant for children, why do they contain maple syrup, liquorice, orange oil and sugar?

◆ In 1997, over 3 million kilograms of methyl bromide, an ozone depleting chemical, was used on tobacco fields worldwide.

◆ An estimated 200,000 hectares of forest are removed by tobacco farming each year. Deforestation occurs mainly in developing countries, amounting to 1.5 per cent of global net losses of forest cover.

◆ It has been estimated that 10 to 20 million people could be fed by food crops grown instead of tobacco.

◆ Many poor countries are entering a phase in which life expectancy has improved because of the control of infectious diseases, but there are now substantial increases in tobacco-related illness, which threaten to reverse this progress.

These are just a few reasons why a **socially conscious generation** may not want to spend their money supporting the tobacco industry. While **peer pressure** is an important factor in children's behaviour, parents can't compete on that field. Our only weapon is the respect we may win for introducing adult themes for discussion.

Comprehending

1. Do you think teenagers might be convinced by any of the arguments against smoking in this article? Support your answer.

2. Do you think this is a well-written article? In your answer, refer to the use of facts and bullet points.

3. In your own words, explain the three expressions written in **bold** print.

TEXTS THAT USE NARRATION

Narrative writing aims to tell stories. It includes travel writing, novels, short stories, biography and autobiography. We are all entertained by stories for their plots, descriptions of characters and places, and the feelings they create in the readers.

In the examination:

● You must be able to say what **kind of story** is being told by the author.

● You must be able to say **how** the story is told.

Features of narrative writing

● Description

● Dialogue

● Atmosphere and mood

The following three extracts are good examples of narrative writing.

≪ T E X T 1 0 ≫

THE KITE RUNNER

This extract from the novel The Kite Runner *by Khaled Hosseini describes the escape of a boy (Amir) and his father (Baba) from Afghanistan during the Russian occupation in the 1980s. The journey out of the country had to be done in secret, as the army and patrols of armed guards were looking for escapees. Here, father and son are being smuggled out in the empty oil tank of a truck.*

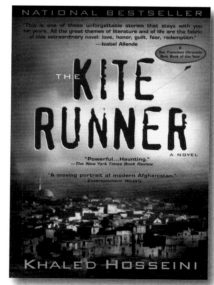

One by one, we mounted the idling truck's rear deck, climbed the rear access ladder, and slid down into the tank. I remember Baba climbed halfway up the ladder, hopped back down and fished the snuffbox from his pocket. He emptied the box and picked up a handful of dirt from the middle of the unpaved road. He kissed the dirt. Poured it into the box. Stowed the box in his breast pocket, next to his heart.

You open your mouth. Open it so wide your jaws creak. You order your lungs to draw air, NOW, you need air, need it NOW. But your airways ignore you. They collapse, tighten, squeeze, and suddenly you're breathing through a drinking straw. Your mouth closes and your lips purse and all you can manage is a strangled croak. Your hands wriggle and shake. Somewhere, a dam has cracked open and a flood of cold sweat drenches your body. You want to scream. You would if you could. But you have to breathe to scream.

The fuel tank was pitch-black. I looked right, left, up, down, waved my hands before my eyes, didn't see so much as a hint of movement. I blinked, blinked again. Nothing at all. The air wasn't right; it was too thick, almost solid. Air wasn't supposed to be solid. I wanted to reach out with my hands, crush the air into little pieces, and stuff them down my windpipe. And the stench of gasoline. My eyes stung from the fumes, like someone had peeled my lids back and rubbed a lemon on them. My nose caught fire with each breath. You could die in a place like this, I thought. A scream was coming.

Coming, coming . . .

And then a small miracle. Baba tugged at my sleeve and something glowed green in the dark. Light! Baba's wristwatch. I kept my eyes glued to those fluorescent green hands. I was so afraid I'd lose them, I didn't dare blink.

Slowly I became aware of my surroundings. I heard groans and muttered prayers. I heard a baby cry, its mother's muted soothing. Someone retched. Someone else cursed. The truck bounced side to side, up and down. Heads banged against metal.

"Think of something good," Baba said in my ear. "Something happy."

Something good. Something happy. I let my mind wander. I let it come.

Comprehending

1. What are the conditions like inside the truck? How does the writer describe these conditions?

2. What do we learn about Baba? Do you think he is a good father?

3. Do you like the way this is told? Give reasons for your answer.

✺ TEXT 11 ✺

THE BOY IN THE STRIPED PYJAMAS

This passage is taken from the novel The Boy in the Striped Pyjamas *set during the Second World War in a concentration camp in Auschwitz. Bruno is a 10-year-old boy whose father is in charge of a concentration camp. A young Jewish boy, Shmuel, and his family are imprisoned there. One day, while walking along the outer fence, Bruno meets Shmuel and they begin an unusual friendship. In this extract, they tell each other of their very different backgrounds.*

"And then one day things started to change," Shmuel expained. "I came home from school and my mother was making armbands for us from a special cloth and drawing a star on each one. Like this." Using his finger he drew a design in the dusty ground beneath him. "And every time we left the house, she told us we had to wear one of these armbands."

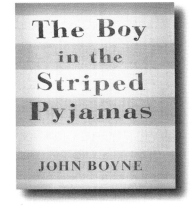

"My father wears one too," said Bruno. "On his uniform. It's very nice. It's bright red with a black-and-white design on it." Using his finger he drew another design in the dusty ground on his side of the fence.

"Yes, but they're different, aren't they?" said Shmuel.

"No one's ever given me an armband," said Bruno.

"But I never asked to wear one," said Shmuel.

"All the same," said Bruno, "I think I'd quite like one. I don't know which one. I don't know which one I'd prefer though, your one or Father's."

Shmuel shook his head and continued with his story. He didn't often think about these things any more because remembering his old life made him very sad.

"We wore the armbands for a few months," he said. "And then things changed again, I came home one day and Mama said we couldn't live in our house any more –"

"That happened to me too!" shouted Bruno, delighted that he wasn't the only boy who'd been forced to move. "The Fury* came for dinner, you see, and the next thing I knew we moved here. And I hate it here," he added in a loud voice. "Did he come to your house and do the same thing?"

"No, but when we were told we couldn't live in our house we had to move to a different part of Krakow, where the soldiers built a big wall and my mother and father and my brother and I all had to live in one room. And not just us," said Shmuel. "There was another family there and the mother and father were always fighting with each other and one of the sons was bigger than me and he hit me even when I did nothing wrong."

"You can't have all lived in the one room," said Bruno, shaking his head. "That doesn't make any sense."

"All of us," said Shmuel, nodding his head. "Eleven in total."

Bruno opened his mouth to contradict him again – he didn't really believe that eleven people could live in the same room together – but changed his mind.

"We lived there for some more months," continued Shmuel, "all of us in that room. There was one small window in it but I didn't like to look out of it because our real home was on the other side of it. And this part of town was the bad part because it was always noisy and it was impossible to sleep. And I hated Luka, who was the boy who kept hitting me even when I did nothing wrong."

"Gretel hits me sometimes," said Bruno. "She's my sister," he added. "And a Hopeless Case*. But soon I'll be bigger and stronger than she is and she won't know what's hit her then."

"Then one day the soldiers all came with huge trucks," continued Shmuel, who didn't seem all that interested in Gretel. "And everyone was told to leave the houses. Lots of people didn't want to and they hid wherever they could find a place but in the end I think they caught everyone. And the trucks took us to a train and the train…" He hesitated for a moment and bit his lip. Bruno thought he was going to start crying and couldn't understand why.

"The train was horrible," said Shmuel. "There were too many of us in the carriages for one thing. And there was no air to breathe. And it smelled awful."

* The Fuhrer: Adolf Hitler.

* Bruno's name for his sister, Gretel.

Comprehending

1. From reading this passage, what do you learn about each of the boys? Pay particular attention to their backgrounds.

2. Why do you think Bruno does not believe everything that Shmuel tells him?

3. Novels are often turned into films. From your reading of this passage, do you think this book would make an interesting film? Base your answer on the above passage.

✑ T E X T 1 2 ✑

FRANKENSTEIN

Frankenstein, by Mary Shelley, was written in the summer of 1816. A group of friends were staying in a villa in France. A thunderstorm made it impossible to go out for days. The friends had a bet to see who could write the scariest novel. One of the results was this famous story.

In the novel, Doctor Frankenstein has been experimenting on corpses, trying to find a way of bringing them back to life. In the following adapted extract, he is shocked by his own success. The English is a little old-fashioned.

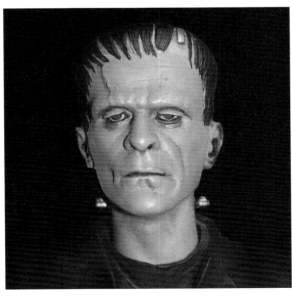

1. It was on a dreary night of November that I beheld the result of all my work. It was already one in the morning; the rain pattered dismally against the panes, and my candle was nearly burnt out, when, by the glimmer of the half-extinguished light, I saw the dull yellow eye of the creature open; it breathed hard, and a movement agitated its limbs.

2. How can I describe my shock at seeing the wretch whom I had worked so hard to create? His limbs were in proportion, and I had chosen features for him I had thought beautiful. Beautiful! Great God! His yellow skin scarcely

covered the mass of muscles and arteries beneath; his hair was of a lustrous black, and flowing; his teeth of a pearly whiteness. These aspects formed a more horrid contrast with his watery eyes, that seemed almost of the same colour as the colourless sockets in which they were set, his shrivelled complexion and straight black lips.

3. I had worked hard for nearly two years, for the sole purpose of putting life into a dead body. For this, I had deprived myself of rest and health. I had desired it more than anything; but now that I had finished, the beauty of the dream vanished, and breathless horror and disgust filled my heart. Unable to endure the sight of the being I had created, I rushed out of the room.

4. For a long time I remained in my bedchamber, walking up and down, unable to sleep. At length, tiredness overcame me and I threw myself on the bed in my clothes, seeking a few moments of forgetfulness. But it was disturbed by the wildest dreams. I thought I saw my beloved, Elizabeth, in the bloom of health, walking in the streets of Ingolstadt. Delighted and surprised, I embraced her; but as I imprinted the first kiss on her lips, they turned the colour of death. Her features appeared to change, and I thought that I held the corpse of my dead mother in my arms; a shroud covered her and I saw the grave-worms crawling in the folds of the cloth. I jumped from my sleep in horror; cold dew covered my forehead, my teeth chattered and every limb shook. Suddenly I saw the creature by the dim and yellow light of the moon, as it forced its way through the window shutters. He held up the curtain, and stared at me. His jaws opened and he muttered some inarticulate sounds, while a grin wrinkled his cheeks. He might have spoken, but I did not hear; one hand was stretched out, seemingly to detain me, but I escaped, and rushed down stairs.

5. Oh! No mortal could bear the horror of that sight. An Egyptian mummy brought back to life could not be as hideous as that wretch.

Comprehending

1. Describe the setting and atmosphere at the beginning of the extract.

2. In your own words, describe the creature that Doctor Frankenstein has created. Support your answer with references to the text.

3. Which of the numbered passages would make the best material for a scene in a film of *Frankenstein*? Give reasons for your answer.

CHAPTER 2
COMPREHENDING
QUESTION B

Question B of Section I in the examination is worth 50 marks. You will be asked to write a short, functional text.

Functional writing requires that you know the correct layout and the best way to present your material. Examples of functional writing include:

- Letters
- Reviews
- Reports
- Memos
- Speeches

It is essential to know your purpose and your audience. These will affect your language and the way that you present your text.

Four Key Questions

- **What** do you wish to say?
- **Who** are you writing for?
- **What** kind of language will you use?
- **What** layout will you adopt?

This chapter contains many examples on which you can model your functional writing exercises. Practice is very important. By the time you finish this chapter, you should have completed several functional writing tasks.

∽ EXAMPLE 1 ∾

LETTER OF COMPLAINT

A letter of complaint is addressed to the management of a restaurant.

Purpose – To complain about the service and quality.
Audience – Manager/owner of the restaurant.
Language – Use clear, plain, impersonal language. Present facts.
Layout – This is a business letter. Make sure to include your address and the address of the business. Date your letter.

```
                                          5 Sands' Row,
                                          Knockadoon,
                                          Co. Down.

The Manager,
Vesuvio,
Fisherman's Quay,
Kinsale,
County Cork.

18 July 2010


Dear Sir or Madam,

I am writing to complain about the poor service I received
last evening — Thursday, 14 July.

This was supposed to be a romantic and unforgettable occasion,
as I had planned to propose to my girlfriend at the end of the
meal. Unfortunately, I will never forget it, for the wrong
reasons. I hold your restaurant to blame for what happened and
I demand satisfaction.

Let me explain.

Earlier in the day I called in to book and make special
arrangements with the staff. The plan was that, when my
girlfriend's dessert was to be served, it would be accompanied
by a violinist and a bunch of flowers. Her dish was to contain
the engagement ring.

What happened was a disaster. When I saw the waiter,
accompanied by the violinist and florist, I got down on my
knees. To my embarrassment, they went to a different table and
I was left looking like a right idiot.
```

Still on my knees, I could hear a woman at another table shouting: "You think a cheap ring, cheesy music and flowers is going to make up for your behaviour?" She proceeded to clatter her unfortunate partner across the face.

I was so upset that I jumped up and in the process upended the table and its contents on top of my poor confused Mel.

The incompetence of your staff is to blame for the worst evening of my life. I want to be compensated for the evening. The dinner cost €150, excluding the flowers and violinist, which were a further €125. Mel's dry cleaning bill is expected to be €50.

I also demand a written apology from your staff. Mel somehow believes that I made a mess of things. I want you to make it clear to her that your staff are entirely responsible for what happened. This might save my relationship.

If a generous offer is not made, I will consider taking legal proceedings against your establishment.

Yours faithfully,
Peter Mooney

Comprehending   I

Question B

Write a letter of complaint. It might concern a product (e.g. a computer or DVD) or a service (e.g. hotel accommodation).

❧ E X A M P L E   2 ❧

DIARY

A diary entry charting the events of a day at the beginning of a school term.

Purpose – To record the events of a day.
Audience – A diary is a private form of writing, but it can be read by others.
Language – Personal, everyday, informal, colloquial language. (Remember to use the present tense about your feelings.)
Layout – Each day must begin with a date. Diary entries are usually written at the end of a day. Use paragraphs to structure your record of the day.

Diary Entry

Friday, 13th September

Not one of my best days. One week back and already the teachers are piling on the pressure. Study plans, career talks, homework schedules, revision periods, and it's all doing my head in. You'd think the Leaving is next week.

I met Geri on the bus this afternoon. Pink hair and funky purple glasses really suit her. She is working in Movieworld, but wants to go back to do the Leaving. She says you need it for the decent jobs. Maybe she should teach career guidance!

After tea, met up with the gang. Seán was in a rotten mood. His folks are making him do Saturday grinds, so he had to be home by eleven. The twins, Mark and Linda, said their parents had imposed an 11.30 curfew. Everybody's parents are getting serious. They must be conspiring. The world is going mad.

Jack, Kate and I tried to get into Crazy Cats Nightclub. The bouncers were strict about ID. So, we went to see a band in the Herb Garden. The name of the band was the Crammers. Great band, what a lousy name!

When I got home, I fell over my school bag, which was in the hall. Maybe that's a sign. Maybe there is no escaping the seriousness of the year.

Mum left out a note: "Recorded that play for you, love." I think she is trying to tell me something.

Looks like I'll just cancel fun this year. Tomorrow I am drawing up a study schedule.

Comprehending

Question B

Write a diary entry supposedly penned by a pupil on the last day of school.

∞ E X A M P L E   3 ∞

FAN LETTER

Purpose – To express admiration.
Audience – The star, celebrity, famous person that you are writing to. You might be aware that a secretary will read the letter first.
Language – The language will be personal, polite and informal. You will want the person to know something about you.
Layout – You must structure this as a letter, so include an address, greeting and date. You can be less formal than in a business letter.

Stephen Duff, a Transition Year pupil, was asked to write a fan letter to someone that he admires. This is his letter.

10 Santry Place,
Dublin 10.
12 September 2010

Dear Mr McShane,

My name is Stephen Duff and I am a Transition Year pupil in a school in Dublin. I play for St John's club and at the moment I am playing for the U16 premier team. I know you used to play for Joey's, who we are due to meet later this month. We're hosting Home Farm on Sunday. I'm a striker myself and have netted a number of goals this season. However, the team is not doing great at the moment.

As a school assignment we have been asked to write to people we admire. I picked you. I was at one of your first games for Ireland against the Czech Republic. You got man-of-the-match. You played brilliantly. You were composed and solid in the middle of the defence. I have since followed your career and have been impressed by your professionalism. I know things have been difficult recently, but I admire your spirit.

I was just wondering if you could visit our club when you are in Dublin. I know you visit your family when you come over for internationals. Maybe you could give us much needed advice on how to defend. If you could it would be brill.

The rest of my class are all writing to rugby players and I'm the only one writing to a soccer player.

Some questions I would really like your answers to:

- What age were you when you went over to England?

- What team picked you up first?

- Who is the best player you have played against?

- Who is the best player you have played with?

25

What preparations do you make before a match?

What is your ambition?

Better go now, thanks for reading.

If you are too busy to visit our training session, I would really appreciate a letter from you.

Yours sincerely,

Stephen

P.S. Best of luck in the league.

Comprehending

Question B

Write a letter to a person you admire. (If you are pleased with your letter, use the Internet to find out how you might send the letter to the person it is intended for.)

∞ EXAMPLE 4 ∞

REPORT

A Fifth Year class was asked to put together a report on the use of computers by pupils in the year. After doing research, the following report was written. Note the layout of this report.

Purpose – To present information about the use of computers in a school and to suggest recommendations.
Audience – The school principal and school management.
Language – The report is impersonal and written in plain language.
Layout – Very formal. Headings, short sections – note the introduction and recommendations.

Introduction: As part of a project on computer literacy, I have undertaken an investigation into the use of computers in my class of 26 pupils.

Our aim was to establish:

- Who has access to a computer.
- What computer skills the pupils have.
- What the computers are being used for.

RESEARCH

- The questionnaire with 20 questions was given to each student.
- Interview with computer studies teacher.

FINDINGS

Access to computer

Twenty-four students had access to a computer at home – of these, 20 have Internet access, but only five have broadband.

All 26 have access to a computer at school, but at very limited times and under strict supervision.

School work

While most students admitted finding the computer useful for Junior Certificate and Transition Year projects, most did not use it for ordinary schoolwork.

Only five students knew that there are websites that offer notes and guides for the Leaving Certificate course.

None of the students use the computer to store school notes. All still use pen and paper.

Entertainment

Not surprisingly, this proved to be the greatest use, with 80 per cent downloading music, 5 per cent downloading films and 90 per cent playing games.

Social life

The phenomenal success of Bebo was one of the many findings.

Nine students have their own sites and all have accessed others' sites.

Little use is being made of e-mail – only three students use it regularly. All stated that texting is more efficient.

Shopping

Out of the 26 students, 11 have bought something on the Internet. This, however, is not a regular occurrence. All stated the same reason – they need to use their parents' credit cards to do so. This was a major bar to using the Internet for shopping.

All expressed the wish to improve their computer skills. They all praised the Computer Studies class they had in Transition Year. They expressed disappointment that no such classes were available in Fifth and Sixth Years.

CONCLUSIONS

Computers are being under-used for schoolwork. There is a need for the computer to be made a more important part of school life.

RECOMMENDATIONS

- Teachers to encourage the use of computers by accepting typed work, using email to notify of homework and setting up a website with notes.
- More classes on computer literacy, so that everybody has at least EDL standard.
- School-funded laptops for all students.

Comprehending I

Question B

Write a report on the activities (sporting, social and cultural) available to students in your school.

☙ EXAMPLE 5 ☙

CURRICULUM VITAE

A student was asked to compile a Curriculum Vitae (commonly called a CV). She was requested to include personal details, and information about her education and interests.

Purpose – To give an account of educational, personal and work-experience details. To impress an employer.
Audience – An employer, personnel department.
Language – Clear and impersonal.
Layout – Presentation is very important. Note the use of headings and short sentences. It is always a good idea to type your CV.

NAME: Kate Purling

DATE OF BIRTH: 16 July 1993

PLACE OF BIRTH: Dublin

ADDRESS: 16, William Street, Ennis, County Clare

SCHOOL: 1998–2003: Ennis Project Primary School
                     2003–9: Limerick County Comprehensive School

                     2009–10: Limerick Post-Leaving Certificate College
                     (Diploma in Tourism and Hospitality Studies).

ACADEMIC RECORD
Leaving Certificate results

Geography	C1
French	C2
Irish	C2
English	C3

WORK EXPERIENCE

- June–August 2009: Ennis Project Summer camp. Organising sports activities for 10 to 12-year-olds.

- June–July 2008: Ennis Healthy-Living Hotel. Taking breakfast orders, occasional reception duties.

- May 2007: Transition Year. Limerick Tourist Office: general office duties, including photocopying and filing. Under supervision, I spent one afternoon helping to place tourists in hotels and offering advice about places and sites to see.

INTERESTS

Travel
I have been to France (on holiday and as an exchange student), Italy, Spain and England.

Reading
I particularly like travel books and fiction about life in different places.

Sport
At school, I played basketball. Recently, I have become involved in tag rugby.

PERSONALITY
Sociable, cheerful, reliable.

ACHIEVEMENTS

- EDL in computer skills.
- First Aid Certificate.
- Driving licence.

REFEREES

Mr Harry Lyre, Solicitor, Prospect Road, Ennis, Co. Clare.
Ms Sue Goodbody, General Manager, Ennis Healthy-Living Hotel, Co. Clare.

Comprehending I

Question B

The following notice appeared in a Sunday newspaper.

**Young person with suitable experience and qualifications
required to work in a newly opened hotel/health centre.**

**Apply Personnel Manager
Nirvana Hotel,
Galway.**

(i)   Compose the letter that Kate Purling might write if she were to apply for this job.

(ii)   Compile your CV and a letter applying for a job for which you consider yourself suitable.

∾ E X A M P L E 6 ∾

A REVIEW

Purpose – To give information and express an opinion. It is usual to recommend or not recommend.

Audience – Those wishing to know about the film. The audience is wide, but remember the age group that the film is intended for.

Language – The language you use should be impersonal. Be aware that you want to be understood by as many people as possible.

Layout – A heading is important. Structure your review into reasonably short paragraphs.

ANGELA'S ASHES

Released in 1999, 145 minutes long, drama.

Starring Emily Watson, Robert Carlyle, Joe Breen, Ciaran Owens, Michael Legge, Pauline McLynn.

Directed by Alan Parker.

Original score by John Williams.

If you enjoy light-hearted romantic comedies, this film is not for you. Based on Frank McCourt's best-selling book about growing up in Ireland during the 1930s, this is a powerful film about the poverty and brutality of an Ireland very different to the one we live in today. Set in Limerick, it is a sad and painful account of growing up.

There are moments of comedy but the mood of depression is present throughout.

The acting is superb. Three young actors are used to play the parts of young Frank McCourt. Scottish actor Robert Carlyle is wonderful as the useless and often drunk father.

The mother, played by Emily Watson, is the real hero. Her life is destroyed by poverty but she never loses her dignity.

This film is highly recommended. Be warned, it is not easy viewing.

MEET THE PARENTS

Released in 2000, 108 minutes in length, comedy.

Starring Robert De Niro, Ben Stiller, Teri Polo, Blythe Danner, Nicole Dehuff, Jon Abrahams.

Directed by Jay Roach.

This is a very funny film.

Male nurse Greg Focker (Ben Stiller) is ready to pop the question to girlfriend Pam Byrne (Teri Polo), but her dear daddy (Robert De Niro), a retired horticulturist, has some old-fashioned ideas about manners and manhood. So, Pam and Greg visit Daddy Byrne's home on Long Island to meet her parents.

From the beginning, the visit is a disaster. One side-splittingly funny incident follows another as Greg reveals himself to be an utter idiot.

The performance of Stiller is outstanding. His expressions are memorable as he makes gaff after gaff. For example, on opening a bottle of champagne, the cork knocks an urn containing the ashes of Grandma Byrne, which end up on the dining room floor being pawed at by the family cat.

Mr Byrne is played fantastically by Robert De Niro. It is soon revealed that he is not just her dad, but is also a CIA agent. Any young man asking for permission to marry his daughter would be intimidated.

This is a must-see film for those who like good old-fashioned slap-stick comedy. See it and have a real laugh. Classic comedy.

Comprehending   I

Question B

Write a review of a DVD or film that you have seen recently. Consider the following points:

- Type (or genre) of film, e.g. thriller, comedy, science-fiction, romantic-comedy, horror.
- The performances given by the actors – mention the names of main actors.
- Short summary of main plot lines.
- Setting.
- What you most liked.
- What you least liked.
- Do you recommend it? To whom?

In your composition, avoid too much use of the first-person singular (e.g. I liked, I loved, etc.).

❧ EXAMPLE 7 ❧

A SHORT SPEECH

Purpose – To give information, instruct and prepare pupils for a school tour.
Audience – It is an audience of young teenagers.
Language – The language is kept simple. Instructions are stated very clearly.
Layout – Introduce oneself and state one's purpose; address the audience in a series of short paragraphs.

This is a speech given to a group of First Year students before going on a school tour.

Good morning, everybody. Today, we are going to the history museum as part of our annual history outing. Mr Perrone, Miss Doyle and I – Mr O'Neill – hope that you will have an interesting day out of school.

Before getting on board the bus, I want you all to line up and give your names to Miss Doyle. Now, I want you to listen very carefully.

As you know, our destination is the history museum. It is a two-hour journey and we will not be stopping. Make sure you do what you have to do before we leave.

On the bus, you may talk quietly to your friends but do not leave your seat. You must have a seat belt on at all times. We don't want our driver getting any penalty points, do we? Our driver needs to concentrate, so you must not make too much noise.

You may eat sweets, but don't litter the bus. Take away with you everything that you bring on the bus. Leave nothing behind.

When we get to the museum, we will be divided into two groups. Those on the left-hand side will be with Mr Perrone. The others will follow Miss Doyle and me.

In the museum, you will need a pencil and something to lean on. If you have phones, keep them either on 'silent' or off.

Now listen closely to my last point. The museum is on a very busy road. Do not cross the road without the permission of a teacher! We want to bring you back in one piece.

Are there any questions? OK, you can all line up in an orderly fashion. We're ready to roll.

Comprehending

Question B

Write a speech addressed to a group of foreign students who are temporarily in your school to improve their English. Offer them useful tips on:

- Life in Ireland.
- Socialising
- Courses.
- Other things to do.

PART II

COMPOSITION

n this section of the book, you will practise writing skills.

Chapter 3

This chapter will give you a chance to revise the important rules of punctuation and grammar. You can also consolidate your spelling skills.

• Remember that the fewer mistakes you make, the better your writing will be.

Chapter 4

This chapter is devoted to the writing of composition. This is the most important section in the Leaving Certificate examination.

• There are sample short stories, articles and speeches in this chapter.

CHAPTER 3

GRAMMAR, SPELLING AND PUNCTUATION

The objective of this chapter is to help the student to write without making mistakes. The first question that students should ask themselves is what mistakes do they make on a regular basis. It is important to identify these in order to avoid repeating them in the examination. Everybody will make different mistakes, though some errors are more commonly made than others.

Think about your most common mistakes and fill in the box below – then begin the chapter.

WHAT MISTAKES DO YOU MAKE ON A REGULAR BASIS?

PUNCTUATION

Punctuation marks make reading easier. These guide us and show when a sentence starts and when it finishes. They also indicate when a person is speaking, when a question is asked and even indicate when a person is angry or being sarcastic.

Read the following paragraph, which is written without punctuation. At first, it is not easy to understand. Can you write it out using the correct punctuation marks?

sean stopped sheila and asked what is the time the time answered sheila its about three but I dont have a watch oh better run then gasped sean thanks its ok replied sheila as sean disappeared

THE FULL STOP

This is used to indicate the end of a sentence.

- Sonya prepared herself for her special date. Her mother told her to be back at 11.30. At nine, Colm arrived in a limo to pick her up. They set off for the party in style.

The stop is sometimes used in certain abbreviations, when words are shortened:

- Monday becomes Mon.
- Thursday becomes Thurs.

The full stop is used in web site addresses:

- www.fbm.com

THE COMMA

This is used to indicate a pause in a sentence.

- Tim and Mary, who had recently married, were working harder than ever to pay the mortgage. Maria was late for the train, but, fortunately, there was a taxi rank on the other side of the road.

It can also be used to separate words in a list:

- The most beautiful counties are Kerry, Cork, Mayo, Sligo, Donegal and Clare.

QUESTION MARK

This is used to indicate the end of a question.

- Is this a question? How do you know?

APOSTROPHE

The apostrophe causes a lot of confusion. There are two main uses.

(a) When there is a letter left out:

- did not *becomes* didn't
- I am *becomes* I'm
- he had *becomes* he'd
- does not *becomes* doesn't
- have not *becomes* haven't

(b) Where there is ownership or possession:

- the castle of the Queen *becomes* the Queen's castle
- the gloves of the goalkeeper *becomes* the goalkeeper's gloves

Remember
When there is more than one person (i.e. plural rather than singular), you put the apostrophe after the 's'.

- the fans of the players *becomes* the players' fans
- the phones of the teachers *becomes* the teachers' phones

CAPITAL LETTERS

ABCDEFGHIJKLMNOPQRSTUVWXYZ

- Always begin a sentence with a capital letter.
- Most acronyms have capital letters, e.g. RTÉ, BBC, NASA.
- Proper names (see box) always begin with a capital letter.

Examples

Places: New York, Spain, Warsaw, Mars, Athlone, India, Skelligs, Isle of Man, Ibiza.

People: Gerry, Vivian, Bob, Ahmed, Miguel, Tony, Carmel, O'Reilly, Soprano, Dylan.

Rivers and mountains: Liffey, Thames, Mississippi, Moy, Everest.

Days and months: Monday, Friday, January, December.

INVERTED COMMAS

- These are used to separate words from the rest of a sentence.
- They are used when you want to show the exact words a person speaks.

Simple rules to follow

Inverted commas are mostly used to show spoken words within a written sentence.

- The actual words spoken go inside the inverted commas.
- A new line for each new speaker.
- Always begin with a capital letter.

Example 1

What time is your train? asked Paula.
"What time is your train?" asked Paula.

I am so sorry that you have to leave, whimpered Hillary.
"I am so sorry that you have to leave," whimpered Hillary.

This is my message to you today! shouted the manager.
"This is my message to you today!" shouted the manager.

Example 2

Where are you going on Friday asked John we are going to France replied Barbara.

"Where are you going on Friday?" asked John.
"We are going to France," replied Barbara.

PUNCTUATION EXERCISES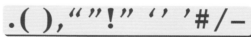

In your copybook, write out these sentences using the correct punctuation marks.

1. have you read dan browns new book asked linda no answered hank why not replied linda ive had no time this summer hank said

2. i have my homework done sir its at home explained michael that's no good to me replied mr jones

3. where do you live asked paul i live in cork replied sile

4. todays newspaper had an unusual headline it simply read no news today

5. what dvds do you have wendy asked laura at the moment only bend it like beckham titanic and kill bill replied wendy

6.   whats that you've got there asked roy its my lucky cat bracelet replied mick your what shouted roy my lucky bracelet I wear it when i play explained mick

7.   julie empied the contents of her bag on the table the policeman saw a phone lipstick some loose change and a credit card whats this he asked its mine she replied i work and i have a card thats not so unusual the policeman picked it up and noticed the name on it david maguire who may I ask is david maguire julie was suddenly quiet

8.   liverpool chelsea and arsenal will qualify from their groups in the champions league suggested big ron do you really think so asked dunphy ron was annoyed by dunphys tone he thought for a moment before replying english clubs have a good record in europe that's rubbish said dunphy teams like ac milan real madrid and barcelona are much better

9.   the principal mr maguire was a soft hearted man he ran his school on three basic principles children were fundamentally good they wanted to learn and cultural activities are good he often told his students and i quote education is what survives when what has been learned has been forgotten

10.   today we are going to begin of mice and men it was written by john steinbeck are you listening to me wendy that was how ms french began class on thursday morning after ten minutes there was chaos some were just talking others were throwing bags out the window while two pupils were actually fighting I felt sorry for her she was always trying to make us interested but i suppose we were not really ready for great american literature

ELIMINATING COMMON MISTAKES

SPELLING

The most common spelling mistakes happen because we confuse words that look or sound alike. Here are the most common ones.

there/their/they're

- Their bags were over there.
- They're on their own over there.

quiet/quite

- Paul is quite quiet today.
- Seán is quiet because he is quite sad about the match.

to/too

- There is too much litter on the street.
- I have to do extra work and it is all too much.

41

accept/except

- Thomas was forced to accept Jill's apology.
- I have seen all of the Bond films, except for one.

break/brake

- He put his foot on the brake just in time.
- The break came in time for the defending team.

advice/advise

- He used to advise me to be careful.
- My father's advice was very good.

principal/principle

- The principal of the school was respected by the pupils.
- On principle, I could not accept the principal demands of his racist programme.

lose/loose

- It was a game that we could not afford to lose.
- The tooth became loose as I ate the apple.

thought/taught

- Larry thought that nothing could go wrong.
- My parents taught me to tell the truth.

affect/effect

- The long, dark winter days affect my mood.
- The half-time talk had a positive effect on the team.

dessert/desert

- My favourite dessert is lemon cheesecake.
- A desert is a difficult place in which to live.

personal/personnel

- I had a personal reason for disliking my tennis coach.
- I sent my application to the personnel department.

threw/through

- I threw the ball for the dog to retrieve.
- I supported my team through the bad times.

weather/whether

- The weather was awful when I was on holiday.
- I don't care whether you were sick or not.

AWKWARD WORDS

Here is a list of words that commonly cause spelling difficulties. Identify those that cause you problems and memorise the correct spellings.

achievement
across
alcohol
amateur
apartment
appearance
argument
athletics
audience
awful

beautiful
beginning
bicycle
biscuit
brilliant
business

captain
changeable
character
clothes
college
coming
commit
comparison
completely
conscience
conscious
continue

deceive
decide
decision
definitely
describe
desperate
develop
disappear
disappoint
disease

economic
efficient

eight
embarrass
emigration
enthusiasm
environment
especially
exaggerate
excellent
existence
experience
extremely

familiar
fascinating
February
finally
foreign
forty

genius
government
guarantee

happiness
height
hero
heroes
hospital
humour
humorous

imagination
immediately
immigration
independent
intelligent
interesting
irrelevant

knowledge

library
licence
license

literature
loneliness
loose
lose
luxury

marriage
meant
medicine
millionaire
minute
mysterious

necessary
noticeable

occasionally
opinion
opportunity

parliament
particularly
personal
personnel
physical
pleasant
politics
politician
possible
practice
practise
prejudice
principal
principle
probably
psychology

queue

really
receive
reference
repetition
restaurant
rhyme

rhythm
ridiculous

sandwich
satisfy
schedule
science
secretary
seize
sense
separate
sincerely
skilful
strength
success
surprise
sympathy

taught
thoroughly
thought
through
tragedy
tragic
truly

unnecessary
until
usually

value
valuable
vicious
villain

Wednesday
wholly
writing

EXERCISES

1. Explain, in your own words, what each of the following mean:

    amateur   conscience   embarrass   emigration   exaggerate   immigration
    millionaire   parliament   prejudice   rhythm   villain

2. Put each of the following words into correct sentences.

    apartment   argument   character   conscious   deceive
    especially   extremely   heroes   immediately   meant
    necessary   opportunity   principal   surprise   usually   vicious

WRITING A PARAGRAPH

A paragraph is a unit of writing in which one point is developed.

Use one sentence to make your point – this is called a topic sentence. Then back up your point with other sentences.

The topic sentence is the most important sentence because it controls the rest of the paragraph.

Study these paragraphs (in each, the topic of the sentence is in bold).

Croke Park is a wonderful stadium. It has a capacity of 85,000. The facilities are state of the art and the pitch is world class. There is nowhere better to be than on Hill 16 watching your county do battle for All-Ireland glory.

September is the saddest month. Summer has well and truly ended and there is a sense of life falling into a routine once again. Days shorten, colours fade and schools open. Throughout the summer, evenings are long and ring out to the sounds of children playing; now, curfews are set and there is work to be done. It is too early to think about Christmas and the pleasures of wintry evenings by the fire.

Jack Temple was odd. His long hair, black suits and runners drew the attention of strangers. He was never seen without his briefcase. In the lapel of his jacket, he always wore something, be it a carnation, rose, dandelion or piece of lettuce. Being in a hurry was his constant state, but what he actually did, no one knew.

The street was quiet. A clock over a chemist showed that it was just after midnight. The windows of the shops reflected no passers by. There was an eerie silence broken only by the sound of a newspaper being rustled by the slight breeze. A black BMW was parked on the corner. The door was open but there was no one in it.

EXERCISES

1. Write one paragraph on each of the following:
   - Advertisements on television.
   - The advantages of having a mobile phone.
   - The best team in the world.
   - A person waiting for a bus.

2. The following sentences contain errors. Write them out without any mistakes. Look out for spelling, grammar and punctuation mistakes.

   When I got their everything was quite. I didn't know what to do.
   There is many difficulties in righting an E-mail.
   I could of scored a goal but their goalie was to good.
   I was holding Barrys place in the cue when I saw you.
   Tom is a friend of yours and he rely cares about you.

CHAPTER 4

COMPOSING

The composition is the most important question on the exam. It is worth 100 marks. This is half of the marks for Paper 1 and one quarter of your total marks in the English examination.

It is important to practise the writing of compositions throughout the year.

In this chapter, you will see many examples of compositions. You should model your compositions on these. Practice will lead to huge improvements in your own writing.

The main kinds of composition are:

- The Personal Essay
- The Short Story
- Article
- Debate or Speech

All compositions should be planned. Do not embark on writing a composition without first thinking about what you want to write and how it should be structured.

The best way of planning a composition is to make a map of your ideas.

APPROACH THE COMPOSITION IN STAGES

STAGE 1: GATHERING IDEAS

Begin by gathering ideas. Use a blank page to write out your ideas.

STAGE 2: BRAINSTORMING

Once you have collected ideas, look over them, considering how they could be developed. What thoughts and memories come to mind? Pick out ideas that you are best able to develop and use in a coherent composition.

STAGE 3: STRUCTURE

Your third step should be to work out a structure for your composition, using the ideas that you have selected. What would make a good introduction? How will you end your piece? What point do you want to make and how best can that be done? Structuring is about turning your ideas into paragraphs.

STAGE 4: WRITE

The final stage is the writing itself. If you have planned properly by selecting good ideas and deciding a structure, the actual writing should flow much more easily. The introduction is particularly important – think of a way to begin the composition that will get the reader's interest.

THE PERSONAL ESSAY

This is writing about a topic that you know very well. It includes your thoughts and ideas on this topic. Try to make your writing interesting and entertaining for the reader. The best compositions are written in an informal and relaxed style. Include plenty of detail about the subject.

TIPS

- Plan.
- Write informally – use everyday language.
- Add some humour.
- Write honestly.
- Add detail and description.

In examining the personal essays in this section, look at the use of paragraphs, the opening and the style.

Points to consider

- Is it well-written?
- Does it keep your attention?
- Is there a structure?
- Can you relate to it?

⌘ S A M P L E E S S A Y 1 ⌘

Read the following account written by a Leaving Certificate student. Her purpose is to describe her relationship with a friend throughout her schooldays.

SCHOOL FRIENDS – MY PERSONAL VIEW

I am looking at a photo of our school trip to Dublin. It was May, two years ago. Eight Transition Year pupils lined up outside the museum. We were supposed to be in uniform. There's Ciara with a belly top, Simon with his hair spiked and gelled, and me, at the back, shielding a nose ring from Miss Noonan's prying eyes. At the front of the photo, Sorcha is staring out with her huge innocent eyes. This photo brings a million memories flooding back.

Sorcha is my best friend. I met her on my very first day in Primary school. I don't remember much about that day. I have been told that I held my mother's hand and was bawling until the teacher had to tear us apart. I was devastated. Another little girl came up to me and handed me her teddy. It was Sorcha. It was our first meeting. Over the years, we have got each other out of so many scrapes.

We sailed through Primary together. We learnt to read and write and do our sums. When she got the measles, I followed within days. We both got bikes for our seventh birthdays and Wendy houses for our eighth. We were mistaken for twins many times. We both cried when Miss Kingston, an American assistant teacher, had to leave at the end of sixth class. For years after, we used to tell each other Miss Kingston's magical stories. When she left, we had a party in the class. Sorcha and I sang a Robbie Williams' song for her.

Secondary school came as a shock to us: homework, heavy school bags and new subjects. Luckily, Sorcha and I were still together. Mr Murphy was our Form teacher in Second Year. He believed every excuse we ever told him. But we never took advantage – at least not too much. Once, Sorcha and I took his sandwiches from his lunchbox and replaced them with a rotten apple and mouldy bread. He pretended nothing happened but the next day he had us cleaning classes during break.

In Transition Year, we had our first taste of work experience. I was sent to a local Primary school and Sorcha to look after children with Down Syndrome. After work, we'd meet up for chips and a milkshake and just talk and talk. Life was simpler then. Our biggest worry was who was going out with whom.

Then she met Jake and I became stupidly jealous. But one night she needed a shoulder to cry on and I am glad it was mine she chose. Jake was never spoken of again.

In Fifth Year, the teachers put on a special disco for the students. It stands out as a special night. It was the first time I really talked to Simon. Up to then, he was the wild boy, always in trouble. That night I learned that he is really quite shy and so sensitive. Although we never became boyfriend and girlfriend, he is a real friend. Sorcha danced with Mr Spain, our Geography teacher. Honestly, that is his name.

In Sixth Year, Sorcha's family moved to Galway. Being separated was a wrench for us both. We promised to text and call. Our friendship proved strong and it lasted. Last Christmas, she invited me to her house and showed me just why Galway is every young person's favourite Irish city.

Now it's May (again) and the dreaded Leaving is in four weeks time. I am working hard as I hope to do a catering course. Sorcha is not sure what to do. We advise each other about our fears, the boys in our lives and the pressure we are under. I really do not think I would survive without her.

As I sit here looking at the photograph taken so many years ago, I have mixed feelings about school. OK, there are always drawbacks like homework and rules – we can't wear makeup – but school has been like a home away from home. I have grown and matured (I hope). I can't wait to leave, but I know I will miss the place. School has given me so much – most of all, my lasting friendship with Sorcha.

Composing

- Using the above composition as a model, write a personal account of your schooldays or your most memorable family moments.

❧ S A M P L E   E S S A Y   2 ❧

This personal essay was written by a Leaving Certificate student. The writer describes her very personal relationship with her mobile phone in an amusing way.

MY PHONE AND ME

There are some things I cannot live without. There are the obvious ones like food, water and air. Friends and family are necessary too. What might shock some people, however, is my devotion to my mobile phone.

My parents gave me my first mobile when I began to be more independent. I was just fourteen. I can still remember the lecture that came with it: "Only use it in emergencies… Ten euro credit a month is all we will get you… keep it switched on so we can be in contact when you are out." My parents are control freaks (like most parents of teenage girls) and they thought that the phone could work for them like those tracking devices that the police attach to convicted criminals.

I quickly learnt the enormous benefits of having one. Need a lift, just speed dial home. There is no taxi service as efficient. Then there is the joy of texting. My teachers often complain about my spelling but I bet no one in the staffroom can use predictive text with my skill.

Since my first phone, I have advanced in leaps and bounds. Each Christmas, I have upgraded my phone. Now I have a camera and Internet access. It's like my own office, devoted to recording my life and keeping me connected with my friends.

Significant things have happened... some I am not proud of. I broke up with a boyfriend a year ago via text. Looking back, I think it was cowardly. Three months later I was dumped by a great guy with a blunt "ur 2 much c u."

My phone and I have been through much together. It has been lost, confiscated, stolen, put in the washing machine, and once it even caused a security alert at an airport. There are so many things it allows me to do: instant organisation of shopping trips with friends; advice on homework; capturing happy moments with the camera.

Most of all, though, I love the privacy and independence it gives me. Our house phone is in the hall, and from the kitchen my mother can hear everything that happens within a hundred metre radius. I only use that phone for basic calls. With my faithful mobile, I can be on a crowded bus but feel alone with loved ones, while in my lonely bedroom I can feel connected to all my friends.

It has been a real saver. I remember my first week in Irish college was hell. I was feeling miserable. I spent a fortune making desperate calls home, begging to be taken away. By the second week, I was adding a whole new set of numbers to my contacts.

The wonderful thing about it is the independence it has given me. My parents needn't worry – just as long as they continue to top up my credit.

Composing |

- Write a personal essay on your most important possession(s). Model your essay on the above example

ᔆ SAMPLE ESSAY 3 ᔆ

In this personal essay, the writer uses the memories of childhood to construct an engaging story.

THE BEST YEARS OF MY LIFE

Looking back on my childhood, there are two summers that really stand out. My parents were going through a difficult time in their marriage and I was sent down to the west coast to spend the long summer holidays with my childless uncle and aunt.

Of course I put up a fight to remain in Dublin with my friends. I had been looking forward to endless football matches, rollerblading and just hanging out. All my protests came to nothing and soon I was on the Galway train heading across the country, going deeper and deeper into the wild-west.

My uncle and aunt tried their best to keep me occupied. I was just not interested in farm life and the weekly trip into the little town. They seemed never to eat anything other than bacon and cabbage. They didn't even have a microwave to put in yummy ready-made meals. Their television could only pick up two stations and the youngest person in the area was 50. I felt I was serving a prison sentence in an old folks home.

Then one day my uncle asked if I would like a job. A friend of his had a couple of boats. I could help out with the lobster pots and with bringing tourists on day trips over to the small island three miles out to sea.

At first I hated it. On my first day, I fell in the water and got soaked when I was trying to pull the heavy pots into the boat. At the end of the first week, my hands were blistered and sore.

Slowly things improved. In the evenings, I was too tired to moan about being bored. I was also too hungry to complain about the food. Instead of thinking about my friends in Dublin and the great time they were having hanging out together, I slept soundly every night.

Mr O'Connor, or Francie as he was called, allowed me the total profits from every fifth lobster and edible crab I caught. This was in addition to the tips I was making from the boat trips to the island. As the summer progressed, business improved and I was saving every cent.

In late July, Francie told me I would be having company. The season was picking up and one person couldn't handle the workload. I was worried. This would mean my share of the profits would go down.

What he hadn't told me was the other worker was his niece from America. She was 16, one year older than me. I couldn't believe my luck.

Scarlet was from Cape Cod. She seemed to know everything about boats and fishing. I will never forget the first day I saw her. I was standing on the pier. Down below me there was a person in the boat, my boat. This person was wearing green Wellington boots, a purple jumper and jeans. Things didn't look too promising. She had her back to me. Then she turned and looked up from the boat. She beamed. "You must be Tommy." I was struck and nearly made my second visit into the water.

She climbed up the iron steps and told me about herself and how she helped her uncle every year.

Together we worked everyday, including Sundays, for the next five weeks. We were a great team. The weeks just rolled by as we ferried and fished and talked and had so much fun together.

On the final week, she asked if I had been to the ceili.

"Of course not", I replied. "I hate that diddly, diddly, fiddly Irish music."

"Well, you're really missing something. Why don't you give it a go? There's one in the village on Saturday. I always go on my last weekend in Ireland."

Saturday evening I was wearing clean clothes for the first time in months. The smell of fish was replaced with lynx and my hair was gelled. Scarlet looked amazing. We had the time of our lives.

I had been to school discos in Dublin but the energy and enthusiasm at this ceili was amazing.

The summer came to an end and I returned to Dublin and Scarlet went back to the States. I am still in contact with Scarlet but who knows when we will meet again.

Composing | 1

- Model a composition on the above. Write a serious or humorous personal account of holidays with your family or write about your best, or worst summer job.

∽ SAMPLE ESSAY 4 ∽

In this essay, the author cleverly introduces the chosen theme – 'Heroes' – by referring to the posters on her bedroom wall. This is a well structured composition and is written with humour.

MY HEROES

Since turning thirteen, three posters have adorned my bedroom walls at different times. First, there was Westlife (I was thirteen), then Ronaldo (hey, I was a fifteen-year-old girl!) and now Bono (at seventeen I am a concerned adolescent). These were/are my teenage idols. However, as I get a little older, I am getting a little wiser – I hope. Next year, I am going to do up my room and I will have no heroes on my walls.

Heroes are people you look up to for inspiration. They are role models. When I think of how Westlife were my heroes, I am a bit embarrassed. There I was, a little thirteen-year-old, singing their songs with the mop as a microphone and the cat and dog as an audience. I would have been one of those embarrassing auditions from the X-Factor.

Then I got interested in football for a while. Ronaldo became my idol. Other footballers just did not compare. My older brother worshipped Wayne Rooney. "That's a real player," he used to say, "Ronaldo is too fancy." But I just could not imagine living in a mansion with Wayne Rooney. Absolutely not.

As I got older, I really got into music. Proper music. Cold Play were my idols. Their catchy songs meant a lot more than other groups. Then my uncle brought me to see a U2 concert. The atmosphere was incredible. I will never forget the feeling when 80,000 people sang along to 'One', the group's anthem. What a song! What a performance! Bono is a real hero. He writes incredible songs and is a spokesperson for poor people in Africa. The anti-poverty campaign is doing real good in the world. Although U2 are very successful, they do not forget about others. I admire the way that they do not behave like spoilt rock stars.

But there are other kinds of heroes. Like a girl in our school who has to struggle with a serious illness. She never complains. Every month she has to go to hospital for a few days. She is never in a bad mood. She has to fight to stay alive. She has shown us how fortunate we are, and how brave she is.

My parents have always been there for me. They are true heroes. They do not have superhuman powers – although I often wonder how my mum manages to do a part-time job, look after three kids, bake, take in stray dogs, keep the house together and manage to have a laugh. My dad makes the dinner every evening, takes care of the garden and helps with the local soccer team every Saturday morning. I do not know where he gets all his energy from.

Writing this has made me realise that there are many kinds of hero.

Composing

- Model a composition on the above. Write a personal account of your heroes or write about what you think of celebrities and stars.

THE SHORT STORY

WHAT MAKES A STORY INTERESTING?

For some readers, it is the theme that makes a story interesting. What themes interest you? Do war, romance, growing up, adventure appeal to you? Other people like stories with characters to whom they can relate. In other words, what interests one person might not hugely interest another. However, certain elements are essential if you are to write an interesting story. This chapter offers advice on all aspects of writing a short story.

It is worth spending time on practising your writing skills. Hopefully, by the end of the chapter, you will be able to write an entertaining story.

FOUR MAIN ELEMENTS

The following elements are essential to a good short story.

- Plot
- Character
- Setting
- Description

PLOT

A plot is a series of events that make up a story. All stories have a **beginning**, **middle** and **end**. In addition, the best plots often have an element of **surprise**. Plots always have a sense of **suspense**; we want to know what happens next.

Shakespeare's play *Romeo and Juliet* has one of the most famous plots.

Beginning

Romeo and Juliet are two young teenagers from two families that are involved in a feud. They meet at a party and fall in love, only realising later that their families are sworn enemies. They make plans to get married in secret.

Middle

Returning to the town square from his secret wedding, Romeo is confronted by Juliet's cousin, Tybalt, his sworn enemy. Romeo is provoked and kills Tybalt. The authorities banish him, giving him 24 hours to leave town. That night, Romeo spends his first and last night with Juliet. The next morning he leaves.

Juliet's parents have a surprise for her. She is to be married to a rich lord. This presents her with a big problem. Another marriage would be a grave sin. She asks the priest who married her to Romeo for advice. He gives her a potion that will put her into a death-like sleep. Believing that she is dead, her family bury in the family crypt. Meanwhile, the priest will notify Romeo who will come to wake her and they can run away together.

End

Word of the priest's plan fails to reach Romeo. Instead, he learns that Juliet has died. He rushes back to die by her side. As he drinks the last bit of poison, Juliet wakes up and sees her dead husband beside her. She stabs herself and they die, side by side.

The families are heart-broken and decide to end their bitter feud. They build two huge statues of Romeo and Juliet to remind everyone of their children's love.

What a story!

Composing

• Write out the plot of a film or play that you have seen. Specify what happens in the beginning, middle and end.

CHARACTER

Interesting characters make interesting stories.

The people in a story should seem real. Try to imagine what they are like – how they dress, how they speak, what they do.

Before writing a story, you should try to imagine your characters as real people.

A grid, such as the one that follows, will prove useful.

Name, age and sex:	Julie, 17, female
Family details:	Younger brother and older sister. Dad drives a taxi and thinks he is a football commentator; mother works in the sports centre, very fit.
Favourite music:	Damien Rice and Amy Winehouse
Clothes:	Tracksuit when not going out; likes to experiment with clothing styles.
Most important possessions:	iPod and mobile; 'Buster' (family pet spaniel); pearl earrings given by grandmother; gym membership card.
Job:	Helps out at animal sanctuary.

You can add more information to develop the character.

Read about these two characters and do similar charts for them.

Eve, 18

- Works part-time in a vet's surgery.
- Her wealthy parents want her to go to New York to work in an art gallery.
- Eve loves to dress in colourful hippy clothes.

Simon, 19

- Part-time worker in a fast food restaurant.
- Plays in a rock group.
- Loves cats.
- His parents have worked hard to give him an education and they are a bit disappointed that he will not give up his music and find a 'proper' job.

Exercise |

- Invent an interesting story in which Eve and Simon meet. Describe the meeting and the problems that they have with family and friends. Describe how they deal with these problems.

- Here are two more story outlines. Chose one that appeals to you and then invent a story.

STORY OUTLINE A

Lucia, 21-year-old Polish woman.
Working in a hotel in Dublin.
Trying to save money to bring her sick brother on a holiday to Ireland from Poland.

Brendan, 55-year-old hotel manager.
He is rude to his foreign workers.
He is very stressed out and the hotel is doing poor business.

Lucia has an interesting idea for the business.
This changes her relationship with Brendan.
The story ends with her brother coming to Ireland on a holiday.

STORY OUTLINE B

Tony, 25-years-old.
Played reserve-team football with Liverpool for a couple of seasons, but a broken leg ended his career.
Now back in Dublin, he has a job at a sports centre.
He refuses an offer from the local amateur team because he is too proud.
Owns an amazing collection of hip-hop CDs.

Laura, a 20-year-old sister of Tony's best friend, Gerry.
She is a big Liverpool fan.
She is a tough young woman with no time for self-pity.
Tends to have trouble with her temper.
Works part-time with disabled children.

USEFUL TIPS

- Pick out one or two physical details – colour of the eyes, hairstyle, etc.

- Describe the clothes. Clothes are a good indication of a person's personality.

- Mention one or two personal items that the person owns. Include something about their family.

- Describe what they are doing and what they are going to do.

- At least one detail should be unusual – everybody is different, after all.

WRITING PARAGRAPHS THAT DESCRIBE A CHARACTER

EXAMPLE 1

Leah Farrell is, to say the least, an unusual 16-year-old. She has a passion for books, does not carry a mobile phone and writes an entry in her diary every day. She adores chips (with ketchup) and never touches healthy food. She always has her homework done and is a very good hockey player. It is surprising that nobody is jealous of her, but she is never called a 'loser' or 'Miss Goody-Two-Shoes'.

In fact, she is the most popular girl in her class. She has a special gift – she makes people laugh.

EXAMPLE 2

Tony Moretti placed his shades on the coffee table and ordered a small cappuccino. He checked his mobile for messages. Scrolling down through the inbox, one caught his attention: *Got it. Meet u @ statue liberty @ 5. Bill.*

This was just what he had been waiting for. Bill had found Dan Brown's manuscript. The last book he had written before his sudden death.

EXAMPLE 3

Jane sat out on the sun-drenched patio. It was 2pm. She had her sunglasses, her MP3, a glass of chilled water and her novel, *Of Mice and Men*. Study and a tan, she thought to herself. Tomorrow's test will be a cinch. She took notes. The afternoon sun climbed higher, the temperature rose. The cat purred loudly under her chair. Within minutes, Jane had nodded off.

The doorbell rang furiously at 3.15pm. Fifteen minutes later, the telephone went into action. Jane slept on.

At 4.10pm, the book clattered to the ground. Jane stirred.

Exercise

- Write a short paragraph, similar in length to those above, that describes a distinct and strong character.

SETTING

All stories take place in specific places. A story-teller must describe this to his or her readers.

Imagine, for example, that you are reading about two teenagers, Brian and Sandra. Brian is a talented musician and Sandra loves athletics. Describe their bedrooms. Below are some useful tips.

- What is on the dressing table? Photographs, CDs, and so on.
- What is the décor like? Are there posters?
- Is the room tidy or untidy?
- What does the window look out upon?
- What object is most important to each person?
- What kind of clothes do they own?

Exercise   I

Describe the following in one paragraph:

1. The scene after a party.
2. The corridor of a school before class begins.
3. A teenager saying goodbye to his/her family as he/she leaves for an exchange.

DESCRIPTION

Good writers vary the words they use. Different verbs can be used to describe the same thing, but with a different emphasis. For example, think of all the verbs that relate to moving and, as an exercise, write them down. You will soon discover that there are more than you thought initially.

USING VERBS

Action words:

- Rachel **went** to school.
- Rachel **walked** to school.
- Rachel **trudged** to school.
- Rachel **skipped** off to school.
- Rachel **sprinted** all the way to school.

What other verbs can be used to describe Rachel going to school?

- Tim **looked** at his watch.
- Tim **glanced** in the window.
- Tim **spied** Judy in the queue.
- Tim **stared** at his mother.
- Tim **spotted** the goalie off his line.

Write out as many sentences as you can, using other verbs for seeing.

The best word is the most accurate and descriptive one.

- Frank **drank** his juice.
- Frank **slurped** his juice.
- Tara **ate** her sandwich.
- Tara **munched** her apple.
- Neasa **scored** a goal.
- Neasa **rocketed** the ball into the net.

Exercise 1

1. Write a paragraph describing two people having dinner together.
2. Write a paragraph describing an exciting sporting moment.
   Use as many different verbs as you can.
3. Fill in the blanks using the words at the end at the exercise.

    (a) Ireland's top model _____ down the catwalk
    (b) The athlete _____ the last 50 metres.
    (c) The Oscar-winning actor _____ onto the stage
    (d) The tourist _____ his suitcases up the road.
    (e) The policeman _____ after the robber.
    (f) The dog _____ across the road.

(*dashed, dragged, pranced, leaped, sprinted, chased*)

4. Fill in the blanks using the list at the end of the exercise.

    (a) Teresa _____ out her message onto the key pad of her phone.
    (b) The boxer _____ his opponent.
    (c) The chef _____ the dough.
    (d) Barry _____ his faithful dog.
    (e) The physiotherapist _____ the athlete's leg.
    (f) Daniel _____ his itchy back.
    (g) Dylan _____ his sore eyes.

(*rubbed, patted, punched, scratched, massaged, pounded, tapped*)

USING ADJECTIVES

Adjectives are words that are used to tell us more about a noun.

- I ate my (*healthy, tasty, small, huge, greasy*) breakfast.
- Wendy got into her (*old, sporty, fashionable, large, vintage, rusty, red, black*) car.
- Gary sat in his (*tidy, untidy, enormous, pokey, dark, bright, damp, sunlit*) room.

'Breakfast', 'car' and 'room' are the nouns that are being described. In these sentences, which adjectives work best in your opinion?

Remember that adjectives help to describe places, people and things.

COLOUR WORDS

Colour words are particularly useful adjectives in descriptive writing.

blue, azure, sky-blue, petrol green, navy
red, scarlet, raspberry, strawberry, pink

Exercise   I

1.   Write out a number of adjectives that describe (i) you, (ii) your room, (iii) a pet, (iv) a sportsperson.

2.   Make a list of as many colour words as you can to describe:
(i)   The sea.
(ii)   The sky.
(iii)   A field.
(iv)   A crowd.

USING ADVERBS

Adverbs help to describe or add to a verb. Look at the following examples, where the adverbs are in **bold**:

- The small man ran **quickly**.
- The old man walked **slowly**.
- The hungry girl ate **voraciously**.
- The strange man stared **rudely**.
- The blue boat sailed **gracefully**.

Do you notice how the adverb changes the meaning of the sentence? Also, from what you learned in the previous section, can you identity the adjectives in these sentences?

Exercise   I

1.   Write out a paragraph on each of the following using adverbs and verbs effectively:
(i)   Pupils arriving for class.
(ii)   Award winners going up to collect an Oscar or MTV award.
(iii)   Christmas shopping.
(iv)   A traffic jam.

2.   Read the following and insert adjectives and adverbs from the list provided.

Matthew was a _____ boy. One _____ morning, while walking _____ to school, he was stopped by a group of _____ first years. They needed help.

One of them had twisted his ankle and needed to be taken to the _____ hospital. Matthew _____ lifted him up and carried him there.

(*nearby, bright, slowly, strong, carefully, frightened*)

3. John Kinsella was an _____ forensic scientist. He thought he had seen everything. One _____ morning, he was called to a _____ wood outside Galway. A _____ corpse had been found. The atmosphere at the crime scene was _____. Gardai sipped their _____ coffees. John was certain that this _____ discovery was going to the first of many.

    (*dark, mutilated, hot, experienced, secluded, eerie, gruesome*)

4. Linda and Cal were _____ in love. They went on _____ walks by the seaside every evening. The _____ summer was coming to an end. Soon they would be back at school, on opposite sides of the country. Linda was heartbroken. Cal swore he would phone and text _____ day. At the bus station, they hugged tightly and _____ said their goodbyes.

    (*fantastic, madly, tightly, tearfully, every, romantic*)

5. Miss Allen was very awkward. Her _____ apartment was full of broken items. Just this morning, while pulling the door shut, the _____ handle came away in her hand. At work, things did not improve. At the _____ coffee machine, she caused a _____ delay when her coins became jammed in the machine. On her way to her work station, she _____ tripped and sent her drink all over the _____ boss. He was completely covered in _____ drinking chocolate.

    (*well-dressed, suddenly, sticky, little, long, busy, metal*)

6. Use accurate verbs, and as many interesting adverbs and adjectives as you can, to describe one of the following situations:

    (i)   A teenager eating his/her favourite dessert.
    (ii)   A sniper preparing to kill.
    (iii) A teenager waiting outside the Principal's office.
    (iv)   A musician on stage.
    (v)   A family dinner.

SAMPLE STORIES

The following are two short stories written by Leaving Certificate students. Read them carefully and then discuss them in class. Before talking about them, read the points below and use them to focus your discussion.

What makes a good story?

- Originality
- Interesting characters
- Description
- Dialogue
- Unexpected ending
- Good vocabulary
- Varied expression

What makes a poor story?

- Boring storylines
- Undeveloped/unbelievable characters
- Dull plots
- Poor/repetitive expression

✑ SAMPLE SHORT STORY 1 ✑

TAKES THE BISCUIT

It was the fifth time that evening that he had put up the tent only to watch it collapse in a heap, like a parachute crumpling to the ground. Dave sighed and muttered under his breath. He felt a cold mark upon his arm and looked up into the ever-darkening sky. Rain. Just what was needed.

Thousands of tents now decorated the field in an explosion of blues, yellows, reds, greens. They were like crazy, overgrown flowers. Rock fans from near and wide had set up camp to attend Ireland's biggest, loudest ever Heavy Rock gathering.

Dave Brogan had been into music since he first heard Guns'n'Roses. This was his dream come true. The next evening he was going to see the band live. But just now he was getting worried about the others. Where had they gotten to?

He knew that it had been a mistake to let Mark bring his friends. They were always trouble. However, he had to make sure they had cover for the night. Working alone, he would make one last attempt to get the tent up. An hour later, and soaked to the skin, he succeeded.

Meanwhile, in town, the other three, Mark, and his friends Wayne and Frank, had been shopping for provisions. Running out of the shop, Frank collided with a stationary Harley Davidson. It wobbled and ever so slowly crashed to the ground. Two bearded Angels fired a barrage of curses at him. The three lads scarpered.

At eight, the four friends were sitting around a stove cooking sizzling sausages and baked beans. It was the first food they had had since setting out at six in the morning. And it was delicious.

Just then the earth shook with the sound of throbbing engines being revved. Six big bikes were criss-crossing the field.

"It's them. Jeez, they must be still mad."

"They'll kill us."

"It's your fault."

"Those things cost thousands. Tens of thousands."

"What are you lot talking about?" asked a completely dumbfounded Dave.

"Oh, in the village this afternoon Frank just, like, destroyed a bike belonging to those hairy death riders on the motorbikes. I read about the Hells Angels. They kill people. And now they must be looking for us."

"You lot hide in the tent."

A moment later a bike earth-quakingly approached. As the visor on the helmet was lifted, a bearded, devilish face yelled.

"Hey, kiddo, did you see three lads your age, one with red hair and a Chelsea shirt?"

"Eh, no." But Dave was the worst liar ever. His face never went along with words. It was like there was a caption written around him that read *I am not telling the truth.*

"Don't mess. I have to find the kid who knocked over my wheels."

But from inside the tent a loud burp popped. Then the Angel blasted his horn and five bikes terrifyingly appeared.

"Look I didn't mean to… I can try and pay… please don't beat us up," pleaded a white-faced Frank as he crawled from the tent.

"What are you talking about? We want to find you because you lot bought the last Crunchy Choc biscuits in the shop. They are the only type Axel eats. We're his handlers. If we don't find them, man, we're dead. I want those biscuits!"

"Here, take them. We've got three packs, take them all."

With that they zoomed off.

At seven the next evening, four bikers came back. As a reward, they took the boys to the back stage area as special guests of the band. Axel signed their t-shirts and treated them as his special guests. He wouldn't, however, share his biscuits.

⊷ SAMPLE SHORT STORY 2 ⊷

BIRTHDAY

On the window sill, a sadly withered rose wilted in its vase. Maggie O'Hara gazed out at the February fields. She was looking out for the little black lamb that had been born one snowy evening the previous week. She was struck by its struggle to survive and its mother's care and attention. Since then the weather had improved. Maggie was tired, she sat down waiting for her relatives to visit.

She was remembering the last time she had seen her family together since her husband's funeral. It must be eight or so years, she thought. Her children had their own lives to get on with.

Mark, she knew, was busy. His job took him all over the country. Last year he clocked up over 50,000 miles. And then there were his children to look after. But wasn't he lucky to have a lovely wife to love him. Larry was in Australia, settled with a wife and three children. When he came home that time, they all went to a fancy restaurant. The whole thing brought family together again, even the youngest, Deirdre. Maggie remembered how Deirdre had always been adventurous, wild. That Christmas dinner had been great until Deirdre took off in a huff. Nobody would tell Maggie what had happened. "You know Deirdre," they had said. "Always has be off somewhere."

A sharp knock at the door shook the memories away.

"Mrs O'Hara, you have a visitor downstairs," said Nurse Nolan.

As the nurse led the soon-to-be 80 year old woman carefully down the stairs, Maggie was sure it was the usual visit from the priest, or the care workers.

But at the bottom of the stairs was a wide-eyed child looking up, calling 'Granny'.

Maggie had never seen the child before. Must be for another inmate, she thought. But she recognised a more familiar face, sitting down in a chair in the hall.

"Deirdre! Well, is it yourself? How are you, love?"

Deirdre arose and embraced her mother, like she did as a child. Especially like when she would hug her mother after being in trouble in school.

"What's wrong, love?"

"Oh, mam, we'd better sit down in the comfy chairs and have a chat."

Sitting down, Deirdre told her mother about her granddaughter. Her little secret. The secret that her siblings had forced her to keep hidden from her mother.

Meanwhile, Annie was allowed out in the garden to play with the nursing home cat.

"Mammy, I want to tell you something and I want you to listen before saying anything."

Deirdre told her old frail mother about life in London. About her divorce. About having a child eight years before.

"Larry and Mark didn't want me to say anything. They said it would upset you. But, mam, I have to let my little Annie see her gran."

Maggie didn't say anything. She pushed herself forward in her chair and with great effort struggled to her feet. She shuffled over to the window and stood staring at the little girl.

"Oh, mam, I am sorry. I shouldn't have come here just to upset you."

"You know she's just like you were at her age." Annie was now running up and down the lawn, doing headstands and returning to pat the cat.

Deirdre noticed a softness in her frail mother's voice. They held hands looking out. "Are you happy? You and Annie. Are you happy?"

"Yes. She is the most beautiful child you could imagine."

"Well then, let's celebrate my eightieth. I want Annie to be my special guest. I'll need help blowing out the candles."

Each of her children received invitations:

Inviting my loving children to celebrate a mother's special birthday.

Saturday 16th March.

That Saturday was the last time the O'Haras would be gathered together, but it was the happiest time for many a year.

Annie met her new cousins and when Mark and Larry saw how happy their mother was, they were happy.

A cake was brought to the table with eight candles.

"My granddaughter, Annie, will be eight next week. She is going to help me blow out the candles. Annie is as much a part of this family as any of you. I love you all."

Maggie O'Hara never had another birthday. A bitterly cold winter had been tough on old people. But she had lived long enough to make sure her family was strong. The funeral was another family celebration, of a life lived with goodness.

Composing

Write a short story inspired by one of the following:

- It all started with a strange text message...
- "This is the six o'clock news. It has been reported that..."
- The limo was outside, but inside the house...
- Losing it.
- The photograph.
- Family secrets.
- The wrong door.
- The mistake.
- The price was right.
- Barriers.
- Dressing up.
- The dating game.
- House rules.
- Getting away.

ARTICLE FOR A MAGAZINE OR NEWSPAPER

Articles for magazines are usually written in a snappy, informal manner. They can give advice and information.

Before writing an article for a magazine or newspaper, you should ask yourself the following questions:

- What kind of magazine or newspaper are you writing for?
- Who is the article written for?
- What information do you want to give?
- What views do you wish to express?

∾ SAMPLE ARTICLE 1 ∾

Read this article, which is written for an audience of Leaving Certificate students and gives information and advice on what they might do for an end-of-school holiday. The article is for a magazine aimed at young people.

LEAVING SCHOOL BEHIND

How are you going to mark your coming of age? The end of secondary school is also the beginning of adulthood. This article sets out some summer options for this year's school leavers.

You will want an enjoyable, but memorable, holiday after all the work you have been doing. Here are some of the things you might like to consider.

The big party in the sun

In the last few years, it has become the in-thing. Pack yourself off to a sun island, usually in Greece, for a week with fellow school-leavers. Crete and Rhodes have become desired locations. You will get plenty of music and fun at an affordable price. Advice: do not drink and swim. And never go into the water after dark. Remember Irish skin is sensitive; bring plenty of sun cream.

Highs: Last chance to be with all your school friends. It's a chance to patch up rivalries and form new friendships. This is a relatively cheap option.

Lows: Do you really want to meet the same old faces? If you didn't get along in the last six years, what's going to change now?

Be warned that teenagers in big groups can be a recipe for disaster. Endless partying does not – believe it or not – appeal to all.

The Interrail trek

One rail ticket, staying in cheap hotels and hostels, visiting major European cities, in a month of frenzied travel. Sound like fun? If it does, then Barcelona, Paris, Rome, Prague, etc., are just waiting for you. This option will appeal to the more culturally aware teenager.

Tips: Budget for a month. Do not stay in 4-star hotels for the first week. Keep a close eye on your belongings in train stations and hostels. This holiday is best done with two or three close friends. Make sure you get along before going.

Highs: Unforgettable experiences. It offers an opportunity to meet new people and to sample other cultures.

Lows: Can be tough for those who do not like to rough it. You will miss home-cooked food.

Music festivals

Chose a number of big festivals around Ireland and Britain – like Oxygen or Glastonbury – and travel to each. You will hear the big names of this generation play live. Be prepared for all weathers. Do not stay out in the sun for a full day without protection. Watch out for illegal substances. You do not know what damage might be done.

Highs: For those who love music, this is the best sort of break. You probably will meet like-minded souls.

Lows: The rain. This is an option only for those who are big into music. The rain. Conditions can be Neanderthal. The rain.

Last family holiday

There is always the last family holiday.

Highs: Cheap option. You have freeloaded for years, why not do so again?

Lows: It is a family holiday. You will be called a loser.

Summer work

There are others who will choose to work for the summer, in order to save for college; leave at least two weeks for a sun break. There are always offers; scan Internet sites.

Highs: You will have something in your account.

Lows: Get a life. There's more to life than money.

Other alternatives

There are individuals who will not be satisfied with any of the above. The more spiritual might want to go to India (be careful of hygiene), surfers who want to experience Hawaii or Australia.

Remember whatever you do should suit you. Make sure you come back safely with plenty of stories for the winter – and years – ahead.

ഏ S A M P L E   A R T I C L E   2 ഏ

The following article is by a Fifth-Year student and deals with the topic of 'respect', arguing that it must be mutual.

RESPECT

Think about it. What a great word.

The Bible says: "Do unto others what you would have them do unto you."

In other words, treat others as you wish to be treated. Show people respect because you wish to be respected.

Young people are always being told to respect the elderly. I am fine with that, but I want to be respected as well.

I like to be different. I dress in a style that some adults consider offensive. I listen to music that has people over 30 running for earplugs. When I visit gran in my (designer) shredded jeans, she makes fun of me. "Why don't you get a nice pair of trousers for yourself?" she says. I don't complain about her ancient cardigans.

My point is that respect is a two-way street. The world would be dull if we were all the same. We should allow everybody the freedom to dress and act as they wish. We are supposed to live in a free society.

Recently, I have become a vegetarian. You wouldn't believe the hassle I get at home. "You'll soon grow out of it" has become "your health will suffer". I try to explain that there is too much cruelty involved in the rearing of animals for slaughter. Nobody in my meat-eating house seems to respect what I believe in.

Does our society tolerate the immigrant, the gay, the traveller amongst us?

In many ways, we have come a long way since the days when outsiders were persecuted. We grant rights to minorities. We are told to respect difference. Unfortunately, this is not always the way we behave.

Ireland has changed in recent years. We are beginning to see that it is important to respect people who come from countries far away. In our school, there are at least ten different nationalities. There are seven different religions being practised by pupils. Young people are better at respecting others. In religion class, we were told that Jesus never turned people away. I think we could learn a lot from this.

Instead of people arguing and fighting over religion, wouldn't the world be a better place if different religions could get along? Sometimes, people act like children fighting over whose dad is stronger, or which team is better. OK, I support Sunderland and we haven't won anything in ages.

Man has harmed the planet we inhabit. We have not shown respect to the earth, the seas, rivers, forests, lakes, animals and plants. I think we should treat this planet as home – you don't mess up where you live, do you? If we don't respect the environment, it will make life difficult for us. I saw the film *Inconvenient Truth* and it showed how we are causing global warming. The lesson is we should respect our planet.

I hope you agree with my views or, if you don't, at least show me respect for having them!

Composing

Write an article on one of the following. Your task is to persuade your readers.

- Saturdays are best spent with friends.

- Sport is a great way of spending free time.

- The joy of keeping pets.

- The importance of school.

- You can learn a lot about a person from the music they listen to.

DEBATE OR SPEECH

In a speech, one presents an argument to an audience in support of, or against, a motion or topic. The speaker's or debater's purpose is to convince the audience – to make the listeners agree with his or her view.

It is essential to 'connect' with the audience.

❧ SAMPLE SPEECH ❧

Here the motion is: **'That Ireland's soul has been sold'**

SPEECH

[Traditional opening.]

Members of the house, chairman, fellow team members and opposition.

[Next, introduce the motion and your view]

We are here today to examine the motion that Ireland's soul has been sold. I agree with this motion. I have three main arguments. Firstly, people today have less time for each other. Secondly, our sense of Irishness is disappearing. And, lastly, we are not living up to the ideals of the patriots who gave their lives for this country.

[The first point is developed.]

I want you to think back to a more simple time in Ireland's history. When our parents and grandparents were growing up, there was a strong sense of community. People looked out for each other. Neighbours shared with each other in bringing up the children. There was no need for crèches. Today we live in vast housing estates. It is not unusual for two parents to be working. They might have to commute to work. This leaves less time in the evenings for social life. It is not uncommon now for people not to know their neighbours. In the past, neighbours looked after each other's children. The old people on the road were watched over by other families.

Nowadays, people move house every few years. We do not build up bonds with each other.

[The second point is developed.]

The second point I want to make is that our Irishness is disappearing. Nearly everybody today speaks English, watches American or British programmes on TV. Be honest, how much Irish music do you listen to? We know more about MTV than RTÉ. The crowd attending a League of Ireland match could fit in a mini-bus, while planes packed with people leave our airports for Premiership games across the channel every Saturday.

I bet that more of you here know more about the characters in Dawson Creek and the OC than you do about the characters in Fair City. How many of you go on foreign holidays? Why do you prefer going to Greece or Spain than to Ireland's resorts? The one thing we have that gives us an identity is the Irish language.

How many in this room speak the language with their friends everyday? I think my point is very clear. We prefer to live without our sense of Irishness.

[The third point is developed.]

My last point is that the leaders of our rebellions fought for an Ireland that would be independent. I think we have abandoned this independence. Since we are part of the EU, we do not make our own decisions. Instead, we have to see what is decided in Brussels. Our currency is no longer our own. For those of you who study Business, you will know that interest rates are set by the Bundesbank in Germany. Patrick Pearse fought in the Easter 1916 rebellion for an Ireland that would be Irish in language and culture. Do we live in that kind of Ireland today?

With our new-found wealth, we dress in Paris fashions and holiday in Spain, speaking English, enjoying foreign food, listening to anything but Irish music on our MP3s.

[Summing up.]

Members of the house, I think you will agree with me. I propose that we do indeed live in an Ireland that has lost its soul.

Composing

1. Present an argument in which you disagree with the above speech. You might consider the following the points.
   - The popularity of the GAA.
   - The success of the Irish language, especially of Irish-speaking schools.
   - Our economy and the advantages of independence.
   - Things to be proud of that are unmistakably Irish.

2. Write a speech on any of the following topics. You may agree or disagree, and remember that your purpose is to convince your audience.
   - Sport is taken far too seriously today.
   - Ireland is a great country in which to grow up.
   - There is more to life than having money.
   - Celebrities are poor role models for our young people.
   - Alcohol should not be sold to people under 21.
   - Young people today are spoilt.

PART III

COMPREHENDING AND COMPOSING EXERCISES

The following chapters are laid out like Paper 1 of the Leaving Certificate examination.

Each chapter is based on a theme (sport, heroes, school etc.)
Texts on the various themes are followed by:
- Comprehending A questions.
- Comprehending B questions.
- Composing questions.

Note

In the Leaving Certificate examination, you will be asked to answer on:
- One of the Comprehending A texts.
- One of the Comprehending B texts
  (the A and B must be answered using <u>different</u> texts).
- One composition.

CHAPTER 5

SPORT

This is an extract from an essay by the writer George Orwell. In it, the writer addresses the negative aspects of competitive sports.

COMPETITION

Nearly all sports practised nowadays are competitive. You play to win, and the game has little meaning unless you do your utmost to win. On the village green, no feeling of patriotism is involved. It is possible to play simply for fun and exercise: but as soon as the question of prestige arises, as soon as you feel that you and some larger unit will be disgraced if you lose, the most savage combative instincts are aroused. Anyone who has played even in a school football match knows this. At the international level, sport is frankly mimic warfare. But the significant thing is not the behaviour of the players but the attitude of the spectators: and, behind the spectators, of the nations who work themselves into furies over these absurd contests, and seriously believe – at any rate for short periods – that running, jumping, kicking a football are tests of national virtue.

As soon as strong feelings of rivalry are aroused, the notion of playing the game according to the rules vanishes. People want to see one side on top and the other side humiliated and they forget that victory gained through cheating or through the intervention of the crowd is meaningless. Serious sport has nothing to do with fair play. It is bound up with hatred, jealousy, boastfulness, disregard of all rules, and sadistic pleasure in witnessing violence: in other words, it is war minus the shooting.

Comprehending

Question A

1. Explain, in your own words, the main argument that George Orwell makes in this article.
2. Which of the visuals at the beginning of Text 1 would you choose to go with this article? Give reasons for your answer.
3. What do the visuals as a group suggest to you about sport? Give reasons for your answer.

Question B

Write out the words of a team talk that a captain or coach might give to his/her players before an important match/event.

⌾ T E X T 2 ⌾

FRANK LAMPARD

This article appeared in the Sunday Times *magazine. It is based on an interview with Frank Lampard, the Chelsea and England footballer. Lampard, at the time, was living in Chelsea with his Spanish fiancée, Elen, and their baby daughter, Luna, and their dog, Daphne.*

The alarm on my mobile is set for 8, but with the baby I'm often already awake. I freshen up, stick on jeans and trainers, let the dog out and get her food. Daphne's a French mastiff. She slobbers a bit, but she's got a beautiful face.

Breakfast is usually a mug of strong English breakfast tea and a bowl of Coco Pops. We get the newspapers delivered, so I usually have a quick flick through and then set off in the car – a blue Aston Martin – for the training ground.

I'll turn on the radio or listen to music. I like U2 and Coldplay. Being in the middle of a season, the sessions aren't too heavy. There are days when it's harder to motivate yourself – you're tired or have things on your mind, but on the whole I enjoy it. I'm a bit of a fitness fanatic, anyway. I got that from my father. He played for West Ham. I wanted to be a footballer for as long as I remember. It was all I thought about. But right from the start, Dad drummed it into me that you have to be fit. By 13, I was good enough to train with two or three professional clubs after school. I was determined to do well in school. I got nine O-levels, including two A's and an A-star. Sometimes I think that if I hadn't made it as a footballer, I'd quite like to have been a lawyer.

Training lasts about an hour and a half, then it's in the shower and lunch. I eat at the grounds where they do things like pastas, salads, meats, chicken and fish. There's not much I don't like when it comes to food. For extra energy I tend to load up with extra carbs a couple of days before a game. After lunch I try to keep my days clear, so I can head back home to Elen and the baby. But I do a bit of charity work and I'm currently involved in the 'Tesco Sport for Schools and Clubs' scheme, which is aimed at inspiring kids to take up sport.

Luna's still only two months old, but I've already bought her first Chelsea outfit with no. 8 on the back. I put it on Luna and when Elen saw her, she said: "She's not going out of the house dressed like that!" I love singing nursery rhymes to Luna.

Sometimes I'll go out shopping. The other day I bought a couple of lovely Yves Saint Laurent suits in Sloane Street. I'm not really into buying the latest gadgets, but I do appreciate something like a good watch. Occasionally, we'll all drive out to the country village, maybe go looking for antiques – I love old furniture.

Elen and I go out for a meal a couple of times a week, but we eat in the rest of the time. Elen mainly does the cooking, but occasionally I'll throw a few bits together – maybe pasta with tomato, chilli and garlic. Normally it comes out okay – not always.

Then we might relax in front of the telly. I love things like the *Sopranos* and confess to getting addicted to things like *Big Brother* and the *X-Factor*.

Before bed I'll let the dog out for a few minutes, set the alarm and then I might read for a while. I recently finished *The Da Vinci Code*, and Roy Keane's autobiography, which was a great insight into the footballer. Sometimes, when I think about all those dreams I had as a kid and where I am now, I have to pinch myself. The hard work, the determination and the sacrifices – they all paid off. Life right now couldn't be sweeter.

Comprehending

Question A

1. What evidence is there that Frank Lampard is a family man? Support your answer by referring to the extract.
2. How important has sport been in his life? Refer to information in the article.
3. Do you think Frank Lampard is a good role model for teenagers? Give reasons for your answer.

Question B

Write out five questions that you would ask Frank Lampard (or any other sportsperson of your choosing) and the answers they might give to your questions.

✺ T E X T 3 ✺

GOLDEN GIRL

An interview with top athlete Niamh O'Sullivan.

When did you first become aware that sport was important to you?
Since the moment I could walk, I began to run. When I was four, I could kick a football and swim. I was a nightmare for my mum because I was always active. There wasn't a time when I didn't play something, but I suppose the turning point was when I won all the athletic medals in my school when I was only 14.

Were there other sports you played at school apart from athletics?
Well, I suppose when you are good at one sport, you tend to be good at most. I loved swimming, but wasn't the best in my class. I loved playing hockey because it is a team sport. There is great fun in being on a team.

Were you good at the academic side of school?
Being honest, no. That said, I was a quiet girl in class. I loved English and History. I would write mad stories that probably were terrible but I loved to write.

If you weren't an athlete, what would job would you have liked?
Something related to sport anyhow. I have a lot of respect for my physios. Maybe a sports journalist or commentator. I like animals and when I was little, I wanted to be a vet.

What are you proud of most?
In sport, my proudest moment was winning the bronze medal at the Olympics. That moment when the flag was raised, I was in tears. However, I am proud of my mother most of all. She had to bring up three children when my father died.

That must have been very tough.
It was. But you can't let things hold you back. I watched my mother struggle and she is an inspiration to me.

What is your normal day like?
When I am training, I get up at 6am. I go for a long run. Breakfast is healthy. I always watch what I eat. I work out in the gym for a few hours. In the afternoon, after a healthy lunch, I do

sprints on the track. My coach works on technique a lot. I finish the session with a long run. Then a healthy dinner. I never eat fast food. I rarely go to bed later than 10pm when I am training. One day a week, I rest. On that day, I only do a 15-kilometre run!

What do you do when you are not training?
I can be a slob. Chilling out in front of X-Factor. Eating a nice meal with my boyfriend. Reading. Simple things. I also like walking in the countryside. I always have a book.

What are your ambitions?
I am focusing on the World Championships at the moment. There are plenty of talented women on the track now and, if I am to win, I will have to be at my best. I also have ambitions for when I retire – I want to help young athletes. I'm also involved with the Special Olympics and that is something I want to give time to.

Most important possessions?
I carry a photo of myself with mum and dad taken when I was three. My phone and iPod are always with me. The thing I value most is my health. Is that a possession?

Have you advice for young athletes?
Believe in yourselves. Train hard. Nobody has won a medal just by being good enough. You have to work hard. Commitment is the most important thing.

Comprehending

Question A

1. Do you think Niamh had a happy childhood? Support your answer by referring to the text.
2. After reading this interview, what kind of person do you think Niamh is?
3. Do you like reading interviews with famous sports stars? Give reasons for your answer.

Question B

Write four or five diary entries describing a typical week in Niamh's life.

COMPOSING

1. 'The importance of sport in my life'. Write a personal account of what sport means to you.

2. Write a speech that you would give to young people in which you encourage them to take up a sport.

3. Write a story based on one of the images in this section.

4. Write about a time when a sporting moment affected you.

5. Write an article for young people on the role played by sporting heroes in our lives.

CHAPTER 6

HEROES

∽ TEXT 1 ∽

The hugely successful television series Lost *has created an interest in its stars. In this article, which appeared in the Saturday magazine section of the* Irish Times, *two of the stars were profiled. Journalist Brian Boyd met them.*

THE PEOPLE WHO CHANGED TELEVISION

Now one of the most watched TV programmes in broadcasting history, *Lost* follows a group of plane-crash survivors on a mysterious island. I got a chance to interview two of its stars.

EVANGELINE LILLY (KATE)

Before *Lost*, Evangeline Lilly's career highlight was playing "a high-school girl leaning against a locker" in a non-speaking role in the 2003 film *Freddy vs. Jason*.

After being cast as Kate, she almost had to turn the role down, as she was having difficulties getting a work visa to enter the US (Lilly is Canadian). In real life, she is engaged to Dominic Monaghan (Charlie).

"I had never really worked in anything before, so the success of show has thrown me. I usually get a few stock reactions from people who recognise me as Kate. The first one is 'I found you' – I get that a lot and you sort of have to laugh even if you want to punch them. The other big one is 'Jack or Sawyer?' or 'Are you scared of flying?' Sitting down beside someone on a plane can be interesting also. Almost everybody wants to know who or what the monster on the island is. I don't know; none of the cast knows yet."

"Playing Kate has changed me as a person. She's brought certain things out of me and changed my way of being. It's hard work, though, I don't think people realise that the episodes are shot just two weeks before they're broadcast."

JORGE GARCIA (HURLEY)

Of all the *Lost* actors, he is the most like his on-screen character in terms of speech patterns, accents and mannerisms. If it weren't for *Lost*, Garcia would be busy with his alternative career choice: a stand-up comedian.

"I've done stand-up stuff on the Los Angeles comedy scene. It's something I would really like to get back to. Would I come and do a gig in Dublin's Comedy Cellar? Sure I would; give me your details."

"The funny thing about me as an actor is that I'm Hispanic – one parent from Cuba, the other Chilean. I'm fluent in Spanish but grew up in the US; because of my name I used to get called to a lot of auditions and when I arrived it would be to read for the part of a Mexican street gang member. The producers would take one look at me and say 'maybe not'."

"I'm well aware of how the name Hurley refers to an Irish sport but that's not the reason why the character got the nickname. Personally, I think he's called Hurley because he's very squeamish – he faints at the sight of blood. Maybe it is to do with hurling up – as in getting sick – but I'm not really sure. It could be another *Lost* mystery."

"The very best thing that has happened to me is that now there is a Hurley action doll in production. The company came to Hawaii to measure me up. Hurley's become a doll – just how cool is that?"

Comprehending

Question A

1. Do you think the two actors' lives have been changed because of the success of the show? Give reasons for your answer.
2. Which of the two actors would you like to meet? Give reasons for your answer.
3. Is this the kind of article that you like to read? Give reasons for your answer.

Question B

Write a review of your favourite television programme. This review is to appear in a magazine for young people.

❧ TEXT 2 ❧

THE BEST YEARS OF OUR LIVES

This is an extract, from an article, written by Sean O'Hagan about the football legend George Best. The article appeared in the Observer *newspaper just after the death of the footballer.*

There were at least two pop songs about him when he was young. I was younger still and, like everyone I knew, in thrall to his genius and glamour. The chorus of one I remember became a terrace chant, audible even in the oddly muffled singing that you heard on *Match of the Day*. It went: "Georgie! Georgie! They call you the Belfast boy!"

That chorus echoed in my heart each time I scored a goal on the patch of scrubby grass in front of my house, right hand raised aloft in triumph like Bestie. I remember it now as a blessed time, distant and unreal. We played on that patch of green until it was worn flat and colourless with our endless to-ing and fro-ing. It was our Old Trafford, and the massed voices we heard singing in our heads when we scored were our Stretford End. "Georgie! Georgie!" they sang, "Georgie, the Belfast Boy!"

Did you know, George, how much we idolised you, loved you, and dreamed of being you or even just meeting you? Did you realise how revered you were by those you left behind, those whose drab, daydream-filled lives you transcended by virtue of your blessedness, your mesmerising genius and transfixing glamour. I doubt it. I suspect it never even crossed your mind.

These thoughts and memories were rattling in my head as I sat in a crowded commuter train trundling out of London last Thursday evening. Everywhere I looked, I saw the headline *GEORGE BEST SLIPS AWAY*.

The Best years of our lives. It is difficult even now, after all this time, to put into words, what George Best meant to those of us who grew up in Northern Ireland amid the rising turbulence of the late Sixties and early Seventies, when he ruled supreme. He was our style icon, our sex symbol and our pop star, all rolled into one. There were times when he seemed like nothing less than a young god.

Comprehending I

Question A

1. In your reading of the opening paragraphs, what did you learn about the writer's childhood? Use references to the extract to support your answer.
2. Why, according to this article, did George Best seem like a 'young god'? Give reasons for your answer.
3. The writer expresses many feelings in this article. How does the writer feel when he hears that George Best has died?

Question B

Write a letter to a famous person that you admire. Tell them why you admire them and explain why you are writing to them.

❧ T E X T 3 ❧

THE CROCODILE HUNTER

This obituary (an account of a person who has recently died) appeared in the Irish Independent.

Steve Irwin was a hyper-enthusiast, thrill-seeking Australian wildlife conservationist who gained a worldwide following with his television show *The Crocodile Hunter*. Last Monday, Irwin was swimming in shallow water off the north-eastern Australian coastline, while filming a documentary, when a stingray's barb tip punctured his heart.

He was following a fleet of the fish when one turned on him and fatally struck – an extraordinarily rare action. The jab from the ten-inch barb of stingray seldom proves lethal. Footage of the incident shows Irwin pulling out the barb, but collapsing in the water. A rescue helicopter lifted him from his boat, *Croc One*, but Irwin was pronounced dead before reaching hospital.

Irwin was known for getting melodramatically near the claws and jaws of dangerous land and sea creatures. He was typically garbed in khaki shorts and short-sleeved shirts, giving him the appearance of an African explorer, and his shaggy blond hair, parted in the middle, gave him a friendly boyish air.

He boasted of hand-feeding the world's most venomous snakes without being bitten. However, a 13-year old female saltwater crocodile once took a large bite from part of his leg, a snack Irwin defended from the animal's perspective: "The poor little female was just defending herself."

Stephen Robert Irwin was born on February 22nd 1962 in Essendon, Victoria, near Melbourne. His parents were amateur naturalists. Irwin spent much of his youth helping his parents nurse injured birds and raise kangaroos. One of his defining early childhood experiences was 'jumping' a crocodile in the Australian outback, with his father's permission. The father/son team caught with their bare hands or bred nearly all the 150 crocodiles at their farm.

He became a household name in Australia for his television series *The Crocodile Hunter* and *Croc Files*. His bravery and sense of humour made him an attractive figure to audiences.

In 1992, Irwin married an Oregon-born naturalist, Terri Raines, who became his filming and writing partner. She and their young children, Bindi, Sue and Robert, survive him.

Stephen Robert Irwin: born February 22nd 1962; died September 4th 2006.

Comprehending

Question A

1. In your own words, describe the kind of man that you think Steve Irwin was.
2. Explain how Steve Irwin died. Refer to the information given in the article.
3. Do you think Irwin is deserving of heroic status? You must support your answer by references to the text.

Question B

Write three or four diary entries in the life of a heroic person. The person can be fictional or real.

☙ T E X T 4 ☙

HEROES

Comprehending

Question A

1. Select the image that best expresses the idea of a hero to you. Give reasons for your answer.
2. Imagine you have been asked to add another image of a hero to this collection. What image would you suggest? Give reasons for your answer.
3. Do you think it is important for young people to have heroes? Give reasons for your answer.

Question B

Write a speech in which you introduce a famous person to an assembly at your school. You should refer to the achievements and character of the person.

1. 'The person (or people) I admire most'. Write a personal essay on this topic.

2. Write a letter to your hero or to a person who has inspired you.

3. Write a story based on any visual in this section.

4. 'In today's world there are no heroes.' Write a speech for a school audience for or against this topic.

5. "The award lay on my desk. I stared at it and thought…" Write a story suggested by this idea.

6. Write an article for a teenage magazine on the importance of role models and heroes in the lives of young people.

CHAPTER 7

SCHOOL

∾ T E X T 1 ∾

This extract is taken from Nick Hornby's novel About A Boy. *Marcus is an unusual 10-year-old, who finds life at school to be quite demanding.*

ABOUT A BOY

He got to school early, went to the form room, sat down at his desk. He was safe enough there. The kids who had given him a hard time yesterday were probably not the sort to arrive at school first thing; they'd be off somewhere smoking and taking drugs and raping people, he thought darkly. There were a couple of girls in the room, but they ignored him, unless the snort of laughter he heard while he was getting his reading book out had anything to do with him.

What was there to laugh at? Not much, really, unless you were the kind of person who was on permanent lookout for something to laugh at. Unfortunately, that was exactly the kind of person most kids were, in his experience. They patrolled up and down school corridors like sharks, except that what they were on the lookout for wasn't flesh but the wrong trousers, or the wrong haircut, or the wrong shoes, any or all of which sent them wild with excitement.

Marcus knew he was weird. When was he going to learn about the singing? He always had a tune in his head, but every now and again, when he was nervous, the tune just sort of slipped out. Anyway, a song had slipped out yesterday during English, while the teacher was reading. This morning he was OK until the first period after break. He was quiet during registration, he avoided people in the corridors, and then it was double maths, which he enjoyed, and which he was good at, although they were doing stuff that he'd already done before.

But then in English things went bad again. They were using one of those books that had a bit of everything in them; the bit they were looking at was taken from *One Flew Over The Cuckoo's Nest*. He knew the story, because he's seen the film with his mum, and so he could see really clearly, so clearly that he wanted to run from the room, what was going to happen.

When it happened it was even worse than he thought it was going to be. Ms Maguire got one of the girls who she knew was a good reader to read out the passage, and then she tried to get a discussion going.

"Now, one of the things this book is about is…How do we know who's mad and who isn't? Because, you know, in a way we're all a bit mad, and if someone decides that we're a bit mad, how do we…how do we show them we're sane?"

Silence.

Ms Maguire was young and nervous and she was struggling, he reckoned. This class could go either way.

"OK, let's put it another way. How can we tell if people are mad?"

Here it comes, he thought. Here it comes. This is it.

"If they sing for no reason, miss."

Laughter. But then it all got worse than he'd expected. Everyone turned around and looked at him; he looked at Ms Maguire, but she had this big forced grin on and she wouldn't catch his eye.

"OK, that's one way of telling, yes. You'd think that someone who does that would be a little potty. But leaving Marcus out of it for a moment."

More laughter. He knew what she was doing and why, and he hated her.

Comprehending

Question A

1. What impression of Marcus do you get from the first two paragraphs?
2. Explain why the other children laugh at Marcus.
3. Do you think this extract is humorous? Give reasons for your answer.

Question B

Imagine that you are Marcus. Write three or four diary entries describing your home and school life.

⋙ T E X T 2 ⋙

Peter Delaney, a Leaving Cert student, wrote this fictional and humorous diary. It gives readers an insight into what study is like for a student.

DIARY OF A SIXTH YEAR

Monday, 6 February: Seafield College 0–Rockbrook 38. Dad was supportive but he had that "I warned you not to get your hopes up look" after the game. Mum is inwardly delighted that (a) I survived the rugby season without facial scarring and (b) now I can concentrate on the Mocks. School was strangely normal. It seems I am the only person who thought we could win. Realised that while I was busy playing rugby all season, others were studying. A lot to do. Next door, Mr Flanagan is at his DIY again. Just finished my first English essay in yonks – 'A Personal Essay on what Sport Means to Me'.

Wednesday, 8 February: Spent last night sorting out my notes. The Leaving Cert must be a major cause of rain-forest depletion. I've really missed the non-rugger friends. Paul stopped by for coffee. He is putting mad hours into his band. He was wondering if I could put my talents to use by helping out with his first gig. That's just what I need – another diversion. Mum thinks he is a bad influence. Girls seem to like him.

Friday, 10 February: Got back my essay. Miss G gave it a B, which is a big achievement. Tonight is Paul's first gig. Gotta go. Promise to study all Saturday

Saturday, 11 February: Paul's gig was great. I did the door, collected €95. Slow start to the day, but I managed a few hours of Maths and Irish. Mum wants me to help with shopping this afternoon. Dad is watching the rugby. Mr Flanagan is continuing to hammer and drill. Haven't seen his missus for a while.

Sunday, 12 February: What is it about work? One week stuck in the books has convinced me that I know almost nothing. This time last week, I was in 'blissful ignorance', as my old history teacher might have said. Flanagan's cat (Roxy) has taken up residence in our kitchen. Where is Mrs F? Paul called over to insist that I become the manager of his band. He has big plans. He thinks getting a C in Economics shows I have the necessary skills. Told him I'd be better off concentrating on studies. "Your decision," he said, as he left. Mr Flanagan was bringing in long planks of wood. Kinda coffin sized! Beginning to think crazy thoughts. What has Mr F done with Mrs F?

Thursday, 16 February: Working well. Haven't seen much of Paul, little of my family, and nothing of Mrs F all week. Roxy is now spending as much time at my desk as I am.

Friday, 17 February: Absolutely wrecked. My training schedule was less tiring than this studying. At last I feel I am making progress. Made out two predictions for LC results.

In one, I was crazily optimistic.

Maths: C
English: C
History: C
Economics: B
Irish: C

Physics: D
French: C

Then, I thought of the worst scenarios: what if my favourite poets don't come up, what if I freeze during the orals, what if Mr F does a full house conversion in the first weeks of June?

Re-did my prediction.

Maths: D
English: E
Economics: D
Irish: D
Physics: E
French: E

I will either be studying in college or putting up posters for Paul. Pressure, pressure, pressure. Getting back to the books.

Saturday, 1 June: Sorry diary, I seem to have lost you sometime in the winter. Just found you this morning after massive clean up of my room. Feeling bad about suspecting Mr Flanagan. It seems his wife went to Liverpool in February to look after her sick sister. While she was gone, Mr F built a new kitchen. What was I thinking? Roxy didn't like the noise.

I am officially a swot. Well pleased with Mocks.

Paul is getting loads of gigs and goes on about how the 'system' doesn't suit him. Ma still doesn't trust him. If I can keep focused, I might be okay in June.

Comprehending I

Question A

1.   Is Peter a typical Leaving Cert student? Use the extract to support your answer.
2.   Did you find Peter's diary interesting to read? Support your answer using references to the extract.
3.   Write Peter's diary entry for the day the Leaving Cert results come out.

Question B

Write a letter to a friend explaining how you are preparing for the Leaving Certificate. Mention whether you are nervous or confident and why you feel this way.

∽ TEXT 3 ∽

THE LESSON

This poem written by Roger McGough offers an unusual view of school life. It raises the question, should there be capital punishment in schools?

Chaos ruled OK in the classroom
As bravely the teacher walked in
The hooligans ignored him
His voice was lost in the din

"The theme for today is violence
And homework will be set
I'm going to teach you a lesson
One that you'll never forget."

He picked on a boy who was shouting
And throttled him then and there
Then garrotted the girl behind him
(The one with the grotty hair)

Then sword in hand he hacked his way
Between the chattering rows
"First come, first severed," he declared
"Fingers, feet, or toes."

He threw the sword at a latecomer
It struck with deadly aim
Then pulling out a shotgun
He continued with his game.

The first blast cleared the back row
(Where those who skive hang out)
They collapsed like rubber dinghies
When the plug's plugged out.

"Please may I leave the room, sir?"
A trembling vandal enquired
"Of course you may," said teacher
Put the gun to his temple and fired

The Head popped a head round the doorway
To see why a din was being made
Nodded understandingly
Then tossed in a grenade

And when the ammo was all spent
With blood on every chair
Silence shuffled forward
With its hands up in the air

The teacher surveyed the carnage
The dying and the dead
He waggled a finger severely
"Now let that be a lesson," he said.

Comprehending

Question A

1.   What elements in this poem are realistic and what are not realistic?
2.   Did you find this a humorous or a menacing poem? Give reasons for your answer.
3.   What lesson does the teacher give the pupils?

Question B

Write a letter to a magazine suggesting ways that school might help students prepare for life.

∽ T E X T 4 ∽

TEACHER MAN

In this extract from his autobiographical account of being a teacher in New York in the 1950s, Frank McCourt recalls his early experiences.

Kids watch, scrutinise, and judge. They know body language, tone of voice, demeanour in general. They absorb it over eleven years and pass it on to coming generations. Watch out for Miss Boyd, they'll say. Homework, man, homework, and she corrects it. She ain't married, so she's nothing else to do. Always try to get married teachers. They don't have time for sitting around with papers and books. Miss Boyd, she sits there at home with her cat and her classical music, correcting our homework, bothering us. Not like some teachers. They give you a pile of homework, check it off, and never even look at it. You could copy out a page from the Bible and they'd write on top, "Very nice."

When did I get the nerve to think I could face American teenagers? Ignorance. That's where I got the nerve.

The door slams against the shelf that runs along the base of the blackboard, stirs a cloud of chalk dust. Entering a room is a big deal. Why couldn't they simply walk into the room, say, Good morning, and sit? Oh, no. They have to push and jostle. One says, hey, in a mock threatening way and another says, hey, back. They insult one another, ignore the late bell, and take their time sitting. Look, there's a new teacher up there, and new teachers don't know nothing. So? Bell? Teacher? New Guy. Who is he? They talk to their friends across the room, lounge in desks too small for them, stick out their legs, and laugh if someone trips. They stare out the window. They gouge their initials on desk tops with penknives, declarations of love with hearts and arrows. Couples sit together, hold hands, whisper and gaze into each other's eyes while three boys against the back closets sing doo-wop, bass, baritone and high notes, man, snap fingers, tell the world they're just teenagers in love.

Comprehending

Question A

1. According to the opening paragraph, why do the pupils not want to have Miss Boyd as their teacher? Do you get the impression she is an effective teacher?
2. From your reading of the passage as a whole, do you think Frank McCourt enjoyed his teaching? Give reasons.
3. Based on this passage, write a diary entry describing Frank's first day teaching in New York.

Question B

Write a speech addressed to First Years, giving advice on how they might settle into their new school.

COMPOSING

1. 'My school days': write a personal account on this topic.

2. Write a short story inspired by one of the texts in this section.

3. Write a speech to be delivered by you to your school friends celebrating the life of a teacher who is about to retire.

4. Write a humorous article for a magazine on the topic, 'Advice to all pupils: How to survive your schooldays'.

5. Write a story in the form of a diary, describing one important week in the life of a pupil. (You should have a separate entry for each day of the week.)

6. Write your views on what you like and do not like about school.

7. 'On the eve of retirement': write a story in which a teacher looks back on his/her teaching days.

Chapter **8**

CHILDHOOD

⌘ TEXT 1 ⌘

This article appeared in the Irish Independent. *It was written by Kim Bielenberg. The article gathered different views about Irish school students.*

SPOILING OUR CHILDREN?

Education Minister Mary Hanafin this week hit out at high-spending school pupils – and their parents. So, are we bringing up a generation of spoilt brats?

She lambasted the youthful obsession with designer labels, X Box computer consoles and binge drinking – mostly paid for with cash from guilt-ridden parents who are too busy to spend time with their offspring.

The degrees to which parents spend money on their children vary enormously, but there is no doubt that Minister Hanafin has struck a chord. Her sentiments are echoed by teachers, parents and young people who have declined to join in the consumer binge.

TWO TEENAGERS RESPOND

- Hazel Nolan, an 18-year-old Leaving Cert pupil from Kinsale, Co. Cork, says she does not fit the minister's image of the over-indulged school pupil. The daughter of a local auctioneer and a former garda inspector may come from a well-to-do family, but she has not been showered with luxurious baubles.

  "You won't see me going around with a Prada handbag. My parents raised me to appreciate the value of things, and most of what I get I work for. When I was 12 years old, I cycled two miles to work as a gardener."

  "I have done babysitting and other work to pay my way. Although I agree with some of what Mary Hanafin says, I think the Government is partly to blame for the way people behave. There is little emphasis in the education system on personal development. All the emphasis is on the Leaving Cert, which is basically a memory test."

- Nick Trigoub-Rotnem, a pupil at a fee-paying school in West Dublin, rejects the notion of cash-rich, spoilt secondary school students.

  "It may be true of a few school pupils in some areas but I believe they are the exception rather than the rule," says Nick, the 18-year-old president of the Union of Secondary Students. "I don't have a car and if I want to go anywhere, it's the public bus. If I want to get money, I'll go out and get a job. Finding work is not as easy as some people may think."

  "As far as parents are concerned, it's all a question of attitude. I know people whose parents are millionaires, but they don't give them everything. Often, it is the parents who are less well-off who give their kids lots of money."

Comprehending

Question A

1. Do you think this article gives a fair and balanced view of Irish children? Support your answer.
2. With which of the views expressed by the two teenagers in this article do you agree? Support your answer by referring to the text.
3. Do you think that teenagers should get part-time jobs to support their lifestyles?

Question B

Write a short article for a magazine in which you agree or disagree with the idea that 'Teenagers should work for their pocket money'.

❧ T E X T 2 ❧

A report on attitudes and behaviour among Irish 12 to 18-year-olds reveals what it was like to be young in Celtic Tiger Ireland. Here are some of the findings of the report.

TIGER CUBS

THE REPORT

77.3 per cent of boys were content with their looks, compared to 53.5 per cent of girls and young women.

60.3 per cent of city girls have a positive body image, compared to 51.9 per cent of girls living in the country.

One-fifth (21.4 per cent) of 12 and 13-year-olds said they were shy, while the figure jumped to 28.9 per cent for 16 and 17-year-olds.

Most (94.7 per cent) own a mobile phone, watch TV every day, listen to music, go to the movies and enjoying 'hanging out' with their peers.

Over a third work part-time weekly or more often, with boys working part-time more frequently than girls.

Disco attendance rises in the 12–18 years group, with young people attending rural schools going to discos more frequently than those in the city.

Girls go shopping weekly, while boys do so less often.

Just over half read in their spare time, with the girls better readers than boys.

During the Leaving Cert year, 60 per cent of young women spent more of their free time studying, compared to 28 per cent of young men.

A large majority (88 per cent) said they were involved in at least one sport.

Soccer, Gaelic football and hurling were most popular for boys, compared to basketball, Gaelic football and swimming for girls.

But, while boys, on average, take part in sport most days, girls take part weekly.

Participation in sports declines for both sexes as they get older, but the drop is more marked for girls.

Almost one-third of boys and a tenth of girls say they never walk for leisure.

Most young people also have one hobby, with just under two-thirds having one or more.

The most popular were playing a musical instrument, looking after pets and art. But far fewer young people are involved in clubs/groups than in sports and hobbies.

Just under one-third are involved with youth clubs, choir and folk groups and scouts or guides.

Most young people believe there is "very little leisure provision" for them in their locality, with young people from rural areas strongest in this belief.

While most young people do not experience financial barriers to leisure activities, 15 per cent said they do not have enough money to take part in the activities they would like to join.

Comprehending | I

Question A

1. What is your overall impression of Irish children from reading this report?
2. What figures most surprise you?
3. "Boys and girls use their time differently." Do you agree with this statement? Support your answer with references to the information supplied in the report.

Question B

Write a letter to a newspaper outlining your views on this report.

∽ T E X T 3 ∽

OUR YOUTH

Comprehending

Question A

1. What impression do these visual images give of young people in Ireland today?
2. Which visual image least represents Irish teenagers? You must give reasons for your answer.
3. What aspect of life in Ireland for a teenager has not been represented by the above visuals and you think should have been? Give reasons for your answer.

Question B

Write a letter to a student living in a foreign country telling them about life in Ireland for a young person.

1.   Write a personal account of your childhood.

2.   Write a short story about an important event in the life of a teenager.

3.   Write a speech in which you talk about the advantages or disadvantages of growing up in Ireland today.

4.   Write an article for a popular magazine in which you address the attraction of shopping centres for young people.

5.   Write a story that begins, "The invitations had been sent out…"

6.   Write an article informing your teenage audience about the best ways to spend the summer.

CHAPTER 9
PREJUDICE AND BULLYING

TEXT 1

Examine this poster and answer the questions below.

RED CARD

Comprehending

Question A

1.   What is the purpose of this poster?
2.   Examine the poster carefully and comment on the use of colour.
3.   Name three places that you would put this poster and explain why you would do so.

Question B

Write a short article that demonstrates the positive contribution that sport makes to society and explain briefly why this increases the impact of the anti-racism message contained in the poster on page 103.

᠕ T E X T 2 ᠕

This is a cartoon produced by the EU to make people aware of prejudice and racism in our society.

Comprehending I

Question A

1. Name the different kinds of prejudice that can be seen in this cartoon.
2. Which illustration do you like most? Give reasons for your answer.
3. Cartoons often have a serious message that they want to get across to the reader. Do you think this cartoon gets its message across? Give reasons for your answer.

Question B

A friend living in a foreign country has written to ask you if there is prejudice in Ireland. Write him/her a letter answering the question.

☙ TEXT 3 ❧

The following article is from Mizz *magazine and was written to coincide with National Anti-Bullying Week in Britain.*

STAND UP TO BULLIES

As it's National Anti-Bullying Week, take five minutes to read our special report and find out how you can stop it from taking place at your school or at home. As it's a very serious issue, get clued up on the facts before you do anything.

What is it?

Bullying takes many different forms. The basic rule is, if someone's behaviour upsets you – especially if it continues when you've made your feelings clear – it is bullying. Examples include unwanted physical contact, teasing, name-calling, spreading nasty rumours or stealing or messing around with a person's possessions. And 'cyber-bullying' – when mobile phones, email or the internet are used to pick on the victim – is a growing problem, too.

If you feel you're being bullied, speak up. It could be as simple as telling a friend she's taking a joke too far, or as serious as getting your head teacher involved. But, whatever you do, don't suffer in silence.

How to get help

If someone is bullying you at school, try to avoid them and surround yourself with friends. If your pals are winding you up, explain to them – or at least to the ones you're closest to – how it makes you feel. If it still doesn't stop, think about finding a new group to hang out with.

Keep a diary at home about what is happening – times and dates may be important. Plus, save any nasty texts or emails you're sent. The best way to get help is to tell your mum, dad, older sister or brother, or another member of your family. You could also tell a teacher you like and trust. By law, your school must treat complaints about bullying seriously and take action to sort them out.

Remember, confiding in an adult doesn't mean they have to take over. Tell them what you'd like to happen – whether it's confronting the bullies or just being aware of a situation in case it gets worse.

If you see someone else being bullied, avoid steaming in because that might make things worse. You may get hurt or accused of being a bully yourself! Instead, talk to the person who's being picked on and see if you can help. Encourage them to talk to an adult, and offer to go along with them for support.

Coping with bullies

Don't let them get to you. Most bullies are unhappy or scared or something, and are taking it out on you. Perhaps someone is bullying them or they're having a tough time at home – not that this is an excuse!

Remember that what's happening is not your fault and you haven't done anything wrong. Bullying can happen to anyone – even celebs aren't immune! ChildLine reported that 23 per cent of their calls last year were about bullying, so don't feel like you're alone.

Don't ignore the bullying – ask someone for help.

Comprehending

Question A

1. According to this article, what is bullying?

2. What advice does the article give to its readers if they are being bullied?

3. Do you think enough is being done to prevent bullying?

Question B

Write three or four diary entries, giving an account of a bullying situation.

COMPOSING

1.   'My views on prejudice'. Write a personal account of your thoughts and feelings on the subject.

2.   "Mum, I am being bullied." Write a short story that begins with this sentence.

3.   Write a speech on the topic, 'Ireland is not a racist country'. You can agree or disagree with the statement.

4.   Write an article about bullying in your school. Find out if there is a teacher who investigates bullying. Interview as many people as you can as part of your research for the article.

5.   Write a story about a person who is starting in a new school and has to find new friends.

CHAPTER 10

VIOLENCE

TEXT 1

Examine these DVD covers and answer the questions below.

Ten years ago some of the worst atrocities in the history of mankind took place in the country of Rwanda and in an era of high-speed communication and round the clock news, the events went almost unnoticed by the rest of the world. In only three months, one million people were brutally murdered. In the face of these unspeakable actions, inspired by his love for his family, an ordinary man summons extraordinary courage to save the lives of over a thousand helpless refugees, by granting them shelter in the hotel he manages.

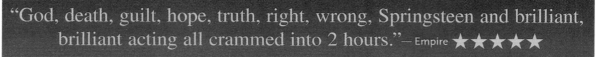

"God, death, guilt, hope, truth, right, wrong, Springsteen and brilliant, brilliant acting all crammed into 2 hours."— Empire ★ ★ ★ ★ ★

Inspired by the true story of a nun's relationship with a condemned man, this provocative examination of crime, punishment and redemption earned Susan Sarandon the 1995 Oscar® for Best Actress and Sean Penn an Oscar® nomination for Best Actor. *Dead Man Walking* is a fast-moving and absorbing film filled with genuine suspense that will leave you awe-struck from beginning to end.

Sister Helen Prejean (Sarandon), a compassionate New Orleans nun, is the spiritual advisor to Matthew Poncelet (Penn), a vicious, angry and complex murderer awaiting execution. Her dedication is to help others, like Matthew, find salvation. But as she attempts to navigate Matthew's dark soul, she encounters a depth of evil that makes her question how far redemption can really go. Can she stave off the fateful day of execution long enough to save Matthew, or will she discover a truth that will rock the very foundation by which she lives her life?

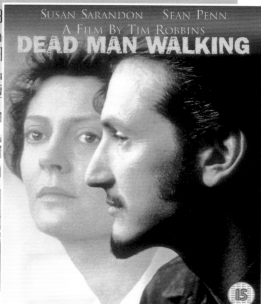

Comprehending

Question A

1. Study the visual aspect of both DVDs. Which visual do you think is the more effective of the two? Give reasons for your answer.
2. Both films deal with difficult subjects. Which film would appeal most to you? Give reasons for your answer.
3. "In far too many films, the violence is excessive." Do you agree with this statement? Refer to films that you have seen.

Question B

Write a short speech to be delivered to your class on the topic, 'The delight or pain of a night out at the cinema'. You may adopt a serious or humorous approach.

∽ T E X T 2 ∽

THE THINGS THEY CARRIED

In this extract from The Things They Carried, *a veteran American soldier, Tim O'Brien, writes about one of his experiences while a soldier in the US army during the Vietnam war.*

When she was nine, my daughter Kathleen asked if I had ever killed anyone. I did what seemed right, which was to say, "Of course not."

I hope, she'll ask again. I want to tell her exactly what happened…

Shortly after midnight we moved into the ambush site outside My Khe. The whole platoon was there, spread out in the dense brush along the trail, and for five hours nothing happened. We were working in two-man teams – one man on guard, while the other slept.

 The night was foggy and hot. For the first few moments I felt lost. I reached out and found three grenades and lined them up in front of me; the pins had already been straightened for quick throwing. And then, for maybe for half an hour, I kneeled there and waited.

Very gradually, in tiny slivers, dawn began to break through the fog. The mosquitoes were fierce. I remember slapping at them, then looking up and seeing the young man come out of the fog. He wore black clothing and rubber sandals and a grey ammunition belt.

He seemed at ease. He carried his weapon in one hand, muzzle down, moving without any hurry up the centre of the trail. There was no sound at all – none that I can remember. In a way, it seemed, he was part of the morning fog, or my own imagination, but there was also the reality of what was happening in my stomach. I had already pulled the pin on a grenade. I had come up to a crouch. It was entirely automatic. I did not hate the young man; I did not see him as the enemy; I did not ponder issues of morality or politics or military duty. I crouched and kept my head low. I tried to swallow whatever was rising from my stomach, which tasted like lemonade, something fruity and sour. I was terrified. There were no thoughts about killing. The grenade was to make him go away – just evaporate. I had already thrown the grenade before telling myself to throw it. The brush was thick and I had to lob it high, not aiming, and I remember the grenade seeming to freeze above me for an instant, as if a camera had clicked, and I remember ducking down and holding my breath and seeing little wisps of fog rise from the earth. The grenade bounced once and rolled across the trail. I did not hear it, but there must've been a sound, because the young man dropped his weapon and began to run, just two or three quick steps, then he hesitated, swivelling to his right, and he glanced down at the grenade and tried to cover his head but never did. It occurred to me then that he was about to die. I wanted to warn him. The grenade made a popping noise – not soft but not loud either – not what I'd expected – and there was a puff of dust and smoke – a small white puff – and the young man seemed to jerk upward as if pulled by invisible wires.

He fell on his back. His rubber sandals had been blown off. There was no wind. He lay at the centre of the trail, his right leg bent beneath him, his one eye shut, his other eye a huge star-shaped hole.

It was not a matter of live or die. There was no real peril. Almost certainly the young man would have passed by. And it will always be that way.

Comprehending   I

Question A

1.   In your opinion, how does Tim O'Brien feel about the experience of killing the soldier? Support your view by detailed reference to the text.
2.   What features of good descriptive writing are to be found in the above passage? Illustrate the points you make with references to the text.
3.   This is a tense scene. Do you think it would be suitable for a film? Give reasons for your answer.

Question B

Write two diary entries that Tim O'Brien might have written describing the days before and after this incident.

❧ TEXT 3 ❧

This is an extract from William Golding's novel Lord of the Flies.

The novel is about a group of boys who are stranded on a deserted island following a plane crash. The boys, whose ages range from 6 to 13, must cope without any help from adults. Ralph has been elected leader. Jack believes he would be a better leader.

LIFE ON AN ISLAND

Ralph was a fair-haired boy.

He was old enough, twelve years and a few months, to have lost the prominent tummy of childhood; and not yet old enough to have made him awkward. You could see that he might make a boxer, as far as width and heaviness of shoulders, but there was mildness about his mouth and eyes that proclaimed no devil.

Jack was tall, thin and bony: his hair was red beneath the black cap. His face was crumpled and freckled, and ugly without silliness.

Ralph cleared his throat. At once he found he could talk fluently and could explain what he had to say.

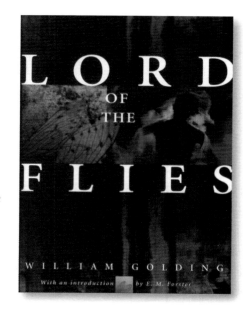

"We're on an island. We've been on the mountain-top and have seen water all around. We saw no houses, no smoke, no footprints, no boats, and no people. We're on an uninhabited island with no other people on it.
There aren't any grown-ups. We shall have to look after ourselves."

The meeting hummed and was silent.

Jack broke in.

"All the same you need an army – for hunting. Hunting pigs –."

Jack slammed his knife into a trunk and looked around challengingly.

Comprehending

Question A

1.   Using your own words, describe the two boys Ralph and Jack.
2.   Which of the two, do you think, would be a better leader? Support your answer.
3.   Suggest five things that the boys should do in order to make survival easier.

Question B

Imagine you are one of the boys. Write three or four diary entries describing your first few days on the island.

∽ TEXT 4 ∽

WELLINGTON

This is a short extract from the opening chapter of the novel The Curious Incident of the Dog in the Night-time *by Mark Haddon. The story is narrated by Christopher, a young boy who suffers from Asperger's Syndrome. He is very logical, but cannot form emotional relationships.*

It was 7 minutes after midnight. The dog was lying on the grass in the middle of the lawn in front of Mrs Shears' house. Its eyes were closed. It looked as if it were running on its side, the way dogs run when they think they are chasing a cat in a dream. But the dog was not running or asleep. The dog was dead. There was a garden fork sticking out of the dog. The points of the fork must have gone all the way through the dog and into the ground because the fork had not fallen over. I decided that the dog was probably killed with the fork because I could not see any other wounds in the dog and I do not think you would stick a garden fork into a dog after it had died for some other reason, like cancer for example, or a road accident.

But I could not be certain about this.

I went through Mrs Shears' gate, closing it behind me. I walked onto her lawn and knelt beside the dog. I put my hand on the muzzle of the dog. It was still warm.

The dog was called Wellington. It belonged to Mrs Shears who was our friend. She lived on the opposite side of the road, two houses to the left.

Wellington was a poodle. Not one of the small poodles that have hairstyles, but a big poodle. It had curly black fur, but when you got close you could see that the skin underneath the fur was a very pale yellow, like chicken.

I stroked Wellington and wondered who had killed him, and why.

Comprehending |

Question A

1. In the opening paragraph, Christopher realises the dog is dead. What leads him to draw this conclusion? Support your answer using reference to the passage.
2. What evidence is there that Christopher is a very observant boy? You must support your answer with references to the extract.
3. What do you like/not like about this passage? Support your answer.

Question B

The police arrived at the scene shortly after Christopher discovered the dog. Imagine you are a detective. Write your report of the crime scene.

COMPOSING

1. Write a story inspired by one of the texts in this section.

2. Write a speech you would give to your class on the topic of violence on television and in films today.

3. Write an article for a newspaper on the subject of violence in our streets.

4. Write a personal account of what books or films mean to you.

5. Write a story that begins "It was a strange case. The only person who could solve the mystery was…"

CHAPTER 11

FAME AND CELEBRITY

WHO WOULD WANT TO BE FAMOUS?

This article appeared in the Sunday Times. *In it, writer AA Gill writes about some of the advantages and disadvantages of being a celebrity.*

Celebrities' lives have become an entertainment commodity. They're there to be stared at and despised.

So, what are the perks of celebrity? Well, you can get a table at a restaurant, which will call the paparazzi, where everyone else will stare at you and demand that you do your catch phrase. Some celebrities are given free handbags, or get to borrow a frock, but they'll have to be photographed in it. You can get an upgrade on an aeroplane and use the lounge. And, through the glass, you can look at the great waves of the *unfamous*, laughing and mucking about, with their bad hair and sloppy bottoms, eating chocolates, pushing prams, never having to look behind them once. A free glass of champagne and an escort to the gate; isn't that a great deal?

But then there's always the money. That must be a solace. Well, actually it isn't. The last myth of stardom is that *everybody who's famous is rich*, that celebrity and wealth are synonymous. Ronnie Barker – comedy star, never off the box – left only £300,000stg. The greatest curse of our time is: "May you be poor and famous." Stars that do make large amounts of money spend ridiculous amounts of it protecting themselves from the rest of us. You have no idea what a cup of Starbuck's coffee, a tabloid and 10 quiet minutes actually costs Catherine Zeta-Jones.

Despite all that, fame is still the number-one ambition of pretty much every kid in the iPod world. Why would anyone want it? To be that vulnerable, to be stalked and mocked, at the beck and call of strangers, to be humiliated and hated by millions of people you've never met, all for precious little?

Comprehending I

Question A

1. According to the writer, what are the "perks of celebrity"?
2. What are the disadvantages of being famous, according to this article?
3. Having read this article, would you like to be a celebrity? You must give reasons for your answer

Question B

Imagine you are hosting a television programme. A famous person has been invited to appear for an interview. Write out a short speech introducing your famous guest to your audience.

∽ TEXT 2 ∾

ARDAL O'HANLON

Ardal O'Hanlon ('Father Dougal' in the famous Father Ted *television comedy) is one of Ireland's best known comedians. This profile of him is taken from a book called* Gift of the Gag, *which is about Irish comedians.*

Ardal O'Hanlon describes himself as a very shy child, who would blush when anybody spoke to him. He grew into an equally bashful teenager, whose rebellion consisted of not making the most of his intellect at school. He describes his upbringing as being rural, pleasant, but a little overprotected. The son of Dr Rory O'Hanlon, later a Fianna Fáil TD and minister, he was sent to boarding school at 13.

His mother, Teresa, shaped his creativity. "I think it was very important to her that we read. She was a bit of a dreamer. We devoured books. I still prefer people who read and go to the cinema and play music – that's the type of company I seek out. I find it very hard to relate to people who are in the money-making business, for example, even though I probably make more than them now"

O'Hanlon is always likeable on stage. He comes across as a bit of a rabbit transfixed in the headlights.

On Fame: "Remember that when I became famous, I was 28, 29. I wasn't star-struck at that age. I was jaded and cynical about everything when I left Ireland. I had no illusions. Fame was not an unwelcome side-effect, but for me it was always about the work. The only thing that has ever been important was the gig, the audience reaction, the gag I wrote that day – did it work?"

This is a typical of his stage show:

"Anyway, my name is Ardal and I come from a very big family. There are 17 of us altogether – well, 15 and two imaginary ones. Of course, there's great respect for a big family in Ireland, isn't there? Especially if they all wear matching clothes made out of felt and walk in single line in descending order of height. And coming from such a big family, you would rarely find us all at the same time in the same place. In fact, I'd say there's only three occasions in life when you'd find the whole family together and they would be a family wedding, or a family funeral, or when I brought home a bag of chips."

Comprehending

Question A

1. Describe Ardal O'Hanlon's background.
2. What kind of person do you think he is?
3. Would you like to be a professional comedian? Give reasons for your answer.

Question B

Write a short review of a television comedy programme.

∽ **TEXT 3** ∾

KATIE MELUA

The singer Katie Melua had an astonishingly fast rise to stardom This article about her appeared in the Sunday Times *magazine. Katie and her producer, Mike Batt, gave an interview to the magazine for the article.*

Consider this. Against all the odds, a girl from the former USSR state of Georgia teaches herself how to write songs, tops the UK charts with her debut album, becomes the biggest-selling artist in Britain for two years running, rejects major-record-label support and a manufactured image.

Melua was born in 1984 in Georgia, when the country was in chaos. Doctors earned less than taxi drivers, so, despite the fact that her father was a heart surgeon, the family had a weekly coupon for a loaf of bread and often lived without heating or hot water. As a child, she watched Eddie Murphy films and *Home Alone*, and gleaned an impression of the West as a place where everyone was happy and shiny and the children had tons of toys.

At nine years old, the family moved to Belfast. The father got a position as a surgeon at the Royal Victoria hospital. "The day we arrived, I remember seeing the terraced houses. I'd never seen houses that close together. I stared with wonder. The most beautiful thing was going to school and being struck by the colours, and that the desks weren't paint-chipped."

The people in Northern Ireland were welcoming and warm. "People have no idea how lucky they are to have been born in the UK," she says. "My view of the future changed so much when I moved. I knew I wouldn't be marrying some bloke at 18 and having kids. I was going to school and thinking about my career at 15; that gave me hope."

After five years in Belfast, the family moved to Redhill, Surrey. At 17, when Melua was studying at the Brit School for Performing Arts and Technology in Croydon, she encountered Mike Batt. He had gone looking for musicians to join a jazz-band project. He scribbled a note at her audition: "Small girl. Good voice. Sang her own song."

He became her producer and mentor.

He boasts that before her debut album was released, she was offered five pages in *Hello!*, but turned it down because it would make her a celebrity rather than a musician.

She tells me that Robbie Williams once called her management company to ask for her phone number. Even though she says he's lovely, she didn't feel right being asked out that way.

"I don't think I could see myself with someone who's famous. I don't like the lifestyle and everything it stands for. It's too superficial. The attention is too much."

Comprehending

Question A

1. Based upon your reading of this article, describe Katie Melua's life up until the time the family went to live in Surrey, England.
2. What is Katie's attitude to fame and celebrity? Do you share her views? Give reasons for your answer.
3. Would you agree that this article gives a positive image of Katie Melua? Give reasons for your answer.

Question B

Imagine you are working for a newspaper or magazine. Write a memo or note to your boss outlining your ideas for an interview with a famous person. Explain why you think this interview would be worth doing. Write out some questions that you would ask.

COMPOSING

1. "It was a long struggle, but I finally achieved my goal." A successful person looks back on their life. Write out the story of how a person achieved their goal.

2. Write an article for a magazine on the people that you think most deserve their success in life.

3. Write a speech on the motion that 'Celebrities are poor role-models for young people'. You may agree or disagree.

4. Write a story in diary form describing a person's rise to stardom.

5. Write a personal account of the people you admire.

CHAPTER 12

FEAR

∞ TEXT 1 ∞

BOB DYLAN

The American songwriter Bob Dylan's memoir, Chronicles, *gives an account of his life. In this extract, he writes about growing up in the 1950s in the United States. At that time, the United States and the USSR were in conflict and many Americans feared a nuclear war.*

In 1951, I was going to grade school. One of the things we were trained to do was to hide and take cover under our desks when the air-raid sirens blew because the Russians could attack us with bombs. We were also told that the Russians could be parachuting from planes over our town at any time. These were the same Russians that my uncles had fought alongside only a few years earlier. Now they had become monsters who were coming to slit our throats and incinerate us. It seemed peculiar. Living under a cloud of fear like this robs a child of his spirit. It's one thing to be afraid when someone's holding a shotgun on you, but it's another thing to be afraid of something that's not quite real. There were a lot of folks around who took this threat seriously, though, and it rubbed off on you. It was easy to become a victim of their strange fantasy.

When the drill sirens went off, you had to lay under your desk, face down, not a muscle quivering and not make any noise; as if this could save you from the bombs dropping. The threat of annihilation was a scary thing. We didn't know what we did to anybody to make them so mad. The reds were everywhere, we were told. Where were my uncles, the defenders of the country? They were busy making a living, working, getting what they could, and making it stretch. How could they know what was going on in the schools, what kind of fear was being roused?

Comprehending

Question A

1. Why were the schoolchildren in the passage trained to take cover under their desks? Support your answer with reference to the passage.
2. Describe, in your own words, what the children were trained to do?
3. What do you think the writer means when he writes "living under a cloud of fear robs a child of his spirit"?

Question B

Write a letter to the newspaper on what you consider to be the greatest threat to mankind today.

❧ TEXT 2 ❧

THE SECRET LIFE OF BEES

*The Secret Life of Bees **written by Sue Monk Kidd** is a novel about a young white girl called Lily. She is growing up in South Carolina in the United States at a time of racial tension. Her mother is dead and she lives with her father T. Ray and Rosaleen, a black servant.*

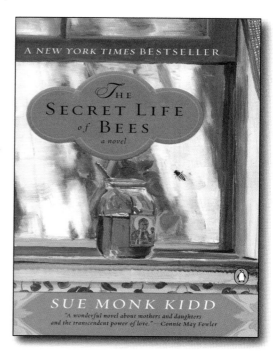

T. Ray and I lived just outside Sylvan, South Carolina; population 3,100. Peach stands and Baptist churches, that sums it up.

At the entrance to the farm we had a big wooden sign with OWENS PEACH ENTERPRISES painted across it in the worst orange colour you've ever seen. I hated that sign. But the sign was nothing compared with the giant peach perched atop a sixty-foot pole beside the gate. Its fleshy colour, not to mention the crease down the middle, gave it the unmistakable appearance of a rear end.

T. Ray didn't believe in slumber parties, which wasn't a big concern as I never got invited to them anyway, but he refused to drive to town for football games, or pep rallies, which were held on Saturdays. He did not care that the clothes I wore I made for myself in home economics class, cotton print shirtwaists with crooked zippers and skirts hanging below my knees, outfits only Pentecostal girls wore. I might as well have worn a sign on my back: *I AM NOT POPULAR AND NEVER WILL BE.*

I needed all the help that fashion could give, since no-one, not a single person, had ever said, "Lily, you are such a pretty child", except for Miss Jennings at church, and she was legally blind.

I watched my reflection not only in the mirror, but in store windows and across the television when it wasn't on, trying to get a fix on my looks. My hair was black like my mother's but basically a nest of cowlicks, and it worried me that I didn't have much of a chin. I kept thinking I'd grow one the same time my breasts came in, but it didn't work out that way. I had nice eyes though, what you would call Sophia Loren eyes.

Comprehending

Question A

1. Why did Lily hate the sign at the entrance to her father's peach farm? Support your answer with references to the text.
2. What evidence is there in the passage that her father was not kind and nice to her?
3. "Lily is a young girl with a poor self-image." Would you agree with this view? You must support your answer by referring to the text.

Question B

Imagine you are Lily. Write a letter to a magazine asking for advice on how to make friends.

☙ T E X T 3 ❧

I'M NOT SCARED

I'm Not Scared, a novel by Niccolo Ammaniti, is set in southern Italy. The main character is a young boy. One day, he and his friends cycle out into the countryside. As a dare, he climbs up a tree to enter an old abandoned farmhouse.

I reached the window without mishap. I looked down. There was a small yard skirted by a row of brambles and the wood behind it pressing in. On the ground there was a cracked cement trough, a rusty crane jib, piles of masonry covered in ivy, gas cylinder and a mattress.

The branch I had to get onto was close – less than a metre away. It was thick and twisty like an anaconda. It would carry my weight. I threw myself arms first, like a gibbon in the Amazon forest. I landed face down on the branch. I tried to grip it, but it was big. I used my legs but there was nothing to get hold of. I started to slip. I tried to claw onto the bark.

Salvation was right in front of me. There was a smaller branch just a few dozen centimetres away. I lunged out and grabbed it with both hands.

It was dry. It snapped. I fell.

I landed on my back. I lay still, with my eyes closed, certain I had broken my neck. I couldn't feel any pain. I lay there, petrified, with the branch in my hands, trying to understand why I wasn't suffering. Maybe I had become a paralytic who, even if you stub out a cigarette on his arm and stick a fork into his thigh, doesn't feel a thing.

I touched the ground with my hands. And I discovered I was on something soft. The mattress.

I moved my feet and discovered that under the leaves, the twigs and the earth there was a green corrugated sheet, a transparent fibre-glass roof. It had been covered up, as if to hide it. And that old mattress had been put on top of it.

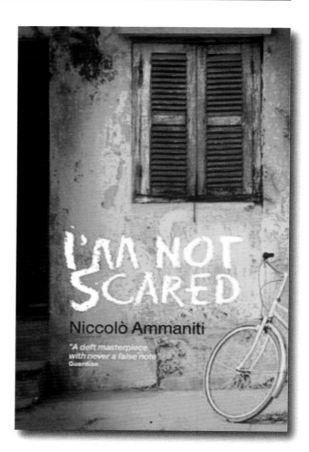

It was the corrugated sheet that had saved me. It had bent and absorbed the force of my fall.

So underneath it must be hollow.

It might be a secret hiding place or a tunnel leading to a cave full of gold and precious stones.

I got down on my hands and knees and pushed the sheet forward.

It was heavy, but gradually I managed to shift it a little. A terrific stink was released. I swayed, put one hand over my mouth and pushed again.

I had fallen on top of a hole.

The walls were made of earth, dug with a spade.

I managed to move it a bit further. The hole was a couple of metres wide and two and a half metres deep.

It was empty.

No, there was something there.

A heap of rolled-up rags?

No…

An animal? A dog? No…

What was it?

It was hairless…

white…

a leg…

a leg!

I jumped backwards and nearly tripped over.

A leg?

I took a deep breath and had a quick look down.

It was a leg.

I felt my ears boil; my head and arms hang heavy.

I was going to pass out.

I sat down, shut my eyes, rested my forehead on one hand, and breathed in. I had to have another look first. I went forward and peered over.

It was a boy's leg. And sticking out of the rags was an elbow.

At the bottom of that hole there was a boy.

He was lying on one side. His head was hidden between his legs.

He wasn't moving.

He was dead.

I stood looking at him for God knows how long. There was a bucket too. And a little saucepan.

Maybe he was asleep.

I picked up a small stone and threw it at the boy. I hit him on the thigh. He didn't move. He was dead. Dead as a doornail. A shiver bit the back of my head. I picked up another stone and hit him on the neck. I thought he moved. A slight movement of the arm.

Comprehending

Question A

1. Describe how the boy loses balance and falls. Support your answer with references to the text.
2. What does he discover in the hole? Refer to the passage in your answer.
3. Do you like the way this story is told? Give reasons for your answer.

Question B

Imagine that the local paper is doing a story on the boy's amazing discovery. Write out the headline and report. You do not need to write more than 150 words.

◈ TEXT 4 ◈

FEAR

Comprehending

Question A

1. Which one of these images, in your opinion, best represents fear?
2. Imagine you were asked to add another image of fear to this collection of images. What image would you suggest? Give reasons for your choice.
3. Write a paragraph explaining your greatest fear.

Question B

Imagine that you have been asked to contribute to a website set up to help young pupils who are afraid of going to secondary school for the first time. Write out the article you would write.

1. Write a personal account of the things that frighten you. You may write about the things that frightened you when you were much younger.

2. Write a story inspired by one of the images in this chapter.

3. Write an article on the interesting fears that people have. This article can be humorous or serious.

4. Write a speech to be delivered to your class on the topic, 'Man is destroying the planet'. You can argue for or against the idea.

5. Write a story that begins: "Fear gripped the nation…"

CHAPTER 13

LOOKING GOOD

DOES BEING SLIM REALLY MATTER?

This article appeared in a magazine. The topic is a very common issue, especially for girls in our society. Two people – the author J.K. Rowling and a magazine columnist – were asked to give their opinions on the issue of being thin. The article was sparked off when Harry Potter author J.K. Rowling branded thin celebrities as "self-obsessed clones", and expressed worries about her three children growing up in a "skinny-obsessed world."

So, should a woman's weight really be an issue?

NO

J.K. Rowling, 40, author

"I've got two daughters who will have to make their way in this skinny-obsessed world, and it worries me because I don't want them to be empty-headed, self-obsessed, emaciated clones.

I'd rather they were independent, interesting, idealistic, kind, opinionated, original and funny – a thousand things, before thin.

Recently, I whiled away part of a journey reading a magazine that featured several glossy photographs of a very young woman who is clearly suffering from an eating disorder. This girl needs help, but the world being what it is, they're sticking her on magazine covers instead.

I mean, is fat really the worst thing a human being can be? Is fat worse than being nasty, jealous, shallow, vain, boring or cruel? Not to me, but then, you might retort, what do I know about the pressure to be skinny?

Being a writer and earning my living using my brain, I'm not in the business of being judged on my looks. But I'd rather my daughters didn't give a gust of stinking Chihuahua flatulence whether the woman standing next to them has fleshier knees than they do."

YES

Carole Malone, 47, columnist

"There's nothing worse than super-thin, super-rich women saying size doesn't matter. Of course it matters. As someone who's spent years yo-yoing between a size 14 and a size 22, I'd say, it's pretty damned important to be slim.

In her rant against our image-conscious society, the size 10 J.K. Rowling says she'd rather her daughters grew up to be interesting and clever, rather than preoccupied with their weight. This is a silly answer. She seems to be suggesting it has to be one or the other.

She says she hates the women she calls 'talking toothpicks' and thinks today's kids are growing up obsessed with thinness.

Well, I'm sorry, people are obsessed with being thin, mainly because society has made sure that being fat isn't fun. We're seen as lazy, greedy, sloppy and untidy. Worse still, obese people are dismissed as weak and out of control.

Try getting clothes to fit if you're fat. Try getting a job if the other applicants are thin and smart. Try meeting a partner. Try getting people to look at you, or listen to what you say. Try being taken seriously when the first thing people notice about you is that your bum's the size of a small country. Life's easier when you're slim – believe me."

Comprehending

Question A

1. Summarise the two viewpoints stated above.
2. With which of the two views are you in most agreement? Give reasons for your choice.
3. Do you think our society is too concerned with how we look? Give reasons to support your view.

Question B

Write a short article for a teenage magazine on the importance of eating healthy food.

☙ T E X T 2 ❧

WILD SWANS

This is an extract from Wild Swans. *This book describes the lives of three generations of women growing up in China during the 20th century. In this extract, the writer tells us about her grandmother who was a child in the 1920s.*

My grandmother was a beauty. She had an oval face, with rosy cheeks and lustrous skin. Her long, shiny black hair was woven into a thick plait reaching down to her waist. She was petite, about five feet three inches, with a slender figure and sloping shoulders, which were considered ideal.

But her greatest features were her bound feet, called in Chinese "three-inch golden lilies". The sight of a woman teetering on bound feet was supposed to have an erotic effect on men, partly because her vulnerability induced a feeling of protectiveness in the onlooker.

My grandmother's feet had been bound when she was two years old. Her mother, who herself had bound feet, first wound a piece of white cloth about twenty feet long round her feet, bending all the toes except the big toe inward and under the sole. Then she placed a large stone on top to crush the arch. My grandmother screamed in agony and begged her to stop. Her mother had to stick a cloth into her mouth to gag her. My grandmother passed out repeatedly from the pain.

The process lasted several years. Even after the bones had been broken, the feet had to be bound day and night in thick cloth because the moment they were released they would try to recover.

For years my grandmother lived in relentless, excruciating pain. When she pleaded, her mother would weep and tell her that unbound feet would ruin her entire life, and that she was doing it for her own good.

Comprehending

Question A

1. In your own words, describe the tradition of foot binding.
2. What reasons are given for mothers wanting to do this to their children?
3. Do women in our society suffer pain, or discomfort, for beauty? What do you think of this?

Question B

Write a letter to the newspaper giving your views on the issue of cosmetic surgery and similar non-essential treatments.

∽ TEXT 3 ∽

GIRL WITH A PEARL EARRING

This novel by Tracy Chevalier is set in Holland in the 17th century. The painter Vermeer has asked his young maid, Griet, to sit for him as he paints her portrait. The painting is now considered a masterpiece and is called the Girl with A Pearl Earring.

He rubbed the swollen lobe between his thumb and finger, and then pulled it taut. With his other hand he inserted the earring in the hole and pushed it through. A pain like fire jolted through me and brought tears to my eyes.

He did not remove his hand. His fingers brushed against my neck and along my jaw. He traced the side of my face up to my cheek, and then blotted the tears that spilled from my eyes with his thumb.

I closed my eyes then and he removed his fingers. When I opened them again he had gone back to his easel and taken up the palette.I sat in my chair and gazed at him over my shoulder. My ear was burning, the weight of the pearl pulling at the lobe. I could not think of anything but his fingers on my neck.

He looked at me but did not begin to paint.

Finally he reached behind him again. "You must wear the other one as well," he declared, picking up the second earring and holding it out to me.

For a moment I could not speak. I wanted him to think of me, not of the painting.

"Why?" I finally answered. "It can't be seen in the painting."

"You must wear both," he insisted. "It is a farce to wear only one."

"But – my other ear is not pierced." I faltered.

"Then you must tend to it."

I got out my needle and clove oil and pierced my other ear. I did not cry, or faint, or make a sound. Then I sat all morning and he painted the earring he could see, and I felt, stinging like fire in my other ear, the pearl he could not see.

And he painted.

When at last he set down his brush and palette, I did not change position, though my eyes ached from looking sideways. I did not want to move.

"It is done," he said. "Take off the earrings and give them back to Maria Thins when you go down."

Now that the painting was finished, he no longer wanted me.

Comprehending

Question A

1. How would you describe the painter? Base your answer on the evidence in this extract?
2. What evidence is there that this was a painful experience for Griet?
3. Examine the painting and the extract. Do you think the writer has been accurate in her description of the scene?

Question B

You have just read an article that criticises young people for spending too much money on clothes and make-up. Write a letter to the magazine giving your opinion on the matter.

❧ T E X T 4 ❧

YOUNG LIVES

Comprehending

Question A

1. What impression of young people is given by these images? Support by referring to the images.
2. Which image do you think best represents young people? Give reasons for your choice.
3. Which image of teenage life least appeals to you? Give reasons for your answer.

Question B

Write a short article about a television programme or film that does/does not give a fair and accurate view of teenage life.

COMPOSING

1. Write a personal account of the importance of clothes to you.

2. Write a story inspired by one of the visuals in this chapter.

3. Write a subject for a young people's magazine giving advice to the readers on the best ways to spend the summer holidays.

4. Write an article giving advice to parents on how to keep their teenagers happy. You may adopt a serious or humorous tone.

5. The motion for your school debate is "Ireland is a young people's paradise". Write out a speech agreeing or disagreeing with the motion.

6. Write a story that begins: "I was young; I was free."

CHAPTER 14

HOME

Sheilstown is a small village in the midlands. This article describes the lives and opinions of some of its inhabitants.

COUNTRY LIFE

PATRICK AND SILVIA WINSTON

Three years ago, Patrick and Silvia and their two children came to live in Sheilstown. They had been living in Dublin, but found the hustle and bustle of life was too much. Silvia was originally from a small town in Italy.

"I like the people here," she says, "They are more friendly and have more time for you than in Dublin. In the shops, you can have a little chat."

She works from home for a publishing company. "I like the freedom this gives me. Once the children are in school, I can go to my office, which is a converted attic, and go online. The only problem is that Internet access can be slow; there is no broadband yet in our area."

Her husband, Patrick, is a teacher in the local school. "I was lucky that a new school opened and I got a job teaching computer studies." They are happy with the amenities in the area. "There is a library and a sports hall with a swimming pool, which is great for the children and ourselves", says Patrick. "The only thing I really miss is real Italian pizza and Italian coffee. Apart from that, life here is great."

BRENDAN AND MARY O'LEARY

Brendan and Mary got married in Sheilstown exactly 50 years ago. They are in their late seventies and have seen many changes.

"I remember when times were tough. My brothers had to go to England and the US to work," says Brendan. "Even my own children had to go to England and Australia in the seventies and eighties."

"There was time when the people around here were really poor. There was no such thing as foreign holidays and no one had a car, never mind two," adds his wife.

They both seem to think that life has improved. Is there anything that was better in the old days?

"People had more time for you in the past. There was always time for tea and a chat. But I suppose there is always a price to be paid for progress," says Brendan.

The O'Leary's are proud of their village. "It's cleaner than in the past. People take care of their houses. I like the new people coming to live here. There are more shops than in the old days," says Mary.

Comprehending

Question A

1.   What are the advantages of living in Sheilstown?
2.   What are disadvantages of living in the village?
3.   Is Sheilstown a place in which you would like to live? Give reasons for your answer.

Question B

Write a letter to a friend in which you describe your feelings when leaving your home place to move to a different town.

∽ T E X T 2 ∽

IMAGINE

This song is one of the most famous by the ex-Beatle member John Lennon.

Imagine there's no heaven
It's easy if you try
No hell below us
Above us only sky
Imagine all the people
Living for today...

Imagine there's no countries
It isn't hard to do
Nothing to kill or die for
And no religion too
Imagine all the people
Living life in peace...

You may say I'm a dreamer
But I'm not the only one
I hope someday you'll join us
And the world will be as one

Imagine no possessions
I wonder if you can
No need for greed or hunger
A brotherhood of man
Imagine all the people
Sharing all the world...

You may say I'm a dreamer
But I'm not the only one
I hope someday you'll join us
And the world will live as one

Comprehending

Question A

1. What image from this song appeals to you most? Give reasons for your answer.
2. From your reading of the lyrics of this song, write a short description of the kind of person that you think John Lennon was.
3. Write out one thing – not mentioned in this song – that would make the world a better place. Give reasons for your choice.

Question B

Write a letter to a person from another country, describing the place you live.

∞ T E X T 3 ∞

PICTURING YOUR HOME PLACE

Comprehending

Question A

1. Choose the image from above that best illustrates your home place. Give reasons for your answer.
2. Write a paragraph describing any of the above images.
3. Which of the images above is least representative of home for you? Give reasons for your answer.

Question B

Compose a short article for a website that informs tourists about your area. You could mention food, cultural and historical attractions.

COMPOSING

1. Write out a personal account of the advantages and disadvantages of living at home.

2. Write a story inspired by one of the images in this chapter.

3. Write a speech in which you address the motion, "The world is our home; it is our duty to keep it clean."

4. Write an article that gives advice to teenagers on how to avoid arguments at home.

5. Write a series of diary entries describing the last week of a teenager's life at home before he sets out for college or work.

6. Write a description of your favourite place or places.

CHAPTER 15
HOLIDAYS

❧ T E X T 1 ❧

PANIC NOT, MOTHER

Gap year students taking a year out after leaving school often travel to far-away places. They keep in touch by e-mail. Here are a few messages sent to calm parents' fears. The selection has been taken from a book compiled by Simon Hoggart and Emily Monk.

E-MAIL 1

I know it's dull to talk about the weather, but it is MINUS 30 degrees today in northern Russia, so I think I am allowed. All my shampoo on my shelf freezes every night and children aren't allowed to go to school because they walk too slowly and might freeze to death before they get there. Nice. I am slightly worried as I walk at the speed of a lobotomized snail. There are five inches of ice on the roads and my new boots have strayed from their natural habitat (of comfy home).

On the first day of unbelievable iciness, I happily stepped outside and within minutes my mascara had frozen my eyelids closed and my nostrils had iced over. After a few minutes I lost all feeling in my fingers and toes, so by the time I reached the Institute I couldn't see, smell or feel. I walk so slowly that I am often overtaken by octogenarian babushkas [grandmothers] shuffling along in felt slippers with massive sacks of turnips on their backs.

Everyday Ludmilla (my flatmate) smugly informs me that it is another 10 degrees colder than the day before and happily informs me how to notice the first stages of frostbite.

E-MAIL 2

We were kitted out in our wetsuits, waterproofs, helmets and lifejackets, and had just started up river (in Peru) when someone started shouting for us to turn the boat and back it up... I turned around to see the body of a dead young woman, not much older than us, floating on the water face up.

Our instructor asked us to grab the body and attach it to the raft. The six of us were all in shock, as it was the first time any of us had ever seen a dead body. Dumbstruck, the only thing we could do was paddle. We got to her side, stood in a circle and said a prayer for her...We carried on rafting and, luckily, all was not ruined, as champagne was brought out to celebrate my birthday and we stayed in a lovely campsite with an excellent view of the mountains.

E-MAIL 3

Esfahan (in Iran) is a tourist city without any tourists. I went to a beautiful medieval mosque one afternoon. It had had six visitors that day. One day, I went to use the computers in the slick new library and decided to use the lavatories in the basement. My Farsi (language spoken locally) isn't up to much, so I couldn't ask directions.

After a while, I found the bathroom and walked in. Imagine my horror as I squatted away in a cubicle and heard the chatter of some women. Here I was in Iran, one of the most sensitive countries on the issue, using the ladies. Chances are the punishment would be something like getting your hands cut off. Iranian ladies are just like the ladies in Europe and America – once they begin chatting they go on forever. So I was trapped for an hour!

E-MAIL 4

To say we were held hostage would be overshooting the mark, although technically it's true. We all went to get the 11am bus into Ghorabi (in Nepal) and, as we approached the place where the bus sits and waits, we were surrounded by six men, none older than us, brandishing 1960s Kalashnikov rifles. They told us to sit down (which we did) and that we were not allowed to leave until the rally was over. We were forced to sit for four hours of political speeches while these Maoists preached their message to the masses. It was scary: they were painfully young and they had guns pointing at us all the time.

When the fear wore off, it got kind of boring. When it was finished, we walked home, and that was that.

Comprehending

Question A

1. Which of these e-mails would a parent least like to receive from a son or daughter? Give reasons for your answer.

2. "Young people are adventurous, but foolish." From reading these e-mails, would you agree with this view of young people? Support your answer by referring to the above e-mails.

3. Outline the advantages and disadvantages of using e-mail to communicate with your family when you are abroad.

Question B

Imagine you are travelling abroad. Write three or four e-mails to your family giving information about your adventures. (You may adopt a serious or humorous tone.)

∽ T E X T 2 ∾

TOP PLACES TO HOLIDAY

The book 1,000 Places To See Before You Die, *written by Patricia Schultz, has become an international bestseller. In the book, information is given about the world's top destinations. Here are some excerpts.*

Mount Etna
Sicily, Italy

Most visitor's first glimpse of Europe's highest and most active volcano – the ancient Greeks called it the Pillar of Heaven – is from the gorgeously sited Greek Theatre in the resort town of Taormina. As long as white smoke rises from Mount Etna's snow capper peak – visible from 150 miles away when not cloaked in mist – all is calm with the world. But too frequently it turns black, stirring restlessness among the area's 1 million residents. These locals continue the centuries-long love-hate relationship with 'muntagna', as they call her in dialect, building and rebuilding their homes perversely close to the volatile mountain. Etna has erupted 300 times since the first recordings 3,000 years ago, most recently in 2001. In one of the most violent eruptions, in 1667, rivers of lava destroyed much of Catania, 19 miles away.

No other gardens in Sicily are as lush as the vineyards and the groves of lemon, orange, almond, and olive trees that today cover the fertile lower slopes leading up to the volcano. But a bus trip that passes through this green belt and continues up to the crater's lip fast becomes a ride through a toasted lunar landscape – brooding, dark, and fascinating. A cable car carries visitors over pinnacles of frozen lava dunes, minor craters, smoke holes – this vision of petrified chaos makes the ascent to Etna's 11,000-feet summit one of Italy's most haunting day trips.

Disney World
Orlando, Florida

Still the pacesetter for theme parks around the globe, Disney World is an ever-expanding universe of make-believe and escapism, celebrating magic, technology, nature and, of course, Mickey Mouse.

In the 30-plus years since it opened its doors, the 30,000-acre former cow pasture has developed into four distinct theme parks, each of which has its own personality.

The Magic Mountain (opened in 1971), the light-hearted fantasy world that revolves around Cinderella's Castle, is home to two of Disney World's most famous attractions: It's a Small World and Space Mountain.

EPCOT (the Experimental Prototype Community of Tomorrow) (opened in 1982) is an educational theme park, where thrills are mostly of the mind, with attractions such as the very popular Spaceship Earth.

At Disney-MGM Studios, visitors can walk onto amazing film sets.

The 500-acre Animal Kingdom is Disney World's largest and newest theme park, with more than 1,000 animals (from giraffes to lions) roaming freely. Themed water parks can also be visited.

Visitors can stay in Disney-owned hotels. The benefits are numerous – they are close to the attractions and are linked by boats, buses and monorail.

Comprehending

Question A

1. Which of the above destinations appeals to you the most? Give reasons for your answer.
2. Which is the least appealing for you? Give reasons for your answer.
3. These extracts come from a book called *1,000 Places To See Before You Die*. Do you think that this would make a good Christmas present for an aunt or uncle? Give reasons for your answer.

Question B

Write a short article describing a place that you think people should visit.

∽ TEXT 3 ∽

LET'S HOLIDAY

Here are four holiday destinations.

Comprehending

Question A

1. Which of these destinations do you find most appealing? Give reasons for your answer.
2. Which do you think is the least appealing? Give reasons for your answer.
3. If you were preparing a brochure for foreign tourists visiting Ireland what image of Ireland would you put on the cover? Describe the image and give reasons for your choice.

Question B

Write a short tourist guide to your locality designed for people your age. Include information on things to do and see. The guide is to be published on a web site.

COMPOSING

1. Write a short story inspired by one of the above places.

2. Write an article giving advice to young people intending to go abroad.

3. Write a personal account of your experience of holidaying with your family. You might like to adopt a humorous approach.

4. Write a story which starts, "At the beginning of the holiday we were best friends …"

5. Write a series of letters/e-mails/blogs giving an account of your stay in a foreign family's house for a week.

6. Write a humorous account of your best and worst moments on holiday.

CHAPTER 16

PETS

CATS OR DOGS

The world seems divided into cat lovers and dog lovers.

First try a little experiment; brainstorm for a moment on the two most popular pets, the cat and the dog. Let me guess:

For the cat you have mystery, Egypt, independence, luxury, sleep, purring, selfishness and comfort.

The dog, on the other hand, brings to mind loyalty, man's best friend, playfulness, giving the paw, barking.

Cats are aristocrats: they prance royally around the house in a superior fashion; they are finicky when it comes to food and they are experts at finding the cosiest corners to rest. Incredible time keepers, they appear mysteriously at meal times and disappear when visitors (especially children) call to the house. Cats adopt people, and keep them as servants, to cater for their every whim. They are independence personified, coming within range of humans only when it suits themselves. Otherwise, they affect an air of self-importance and indifference.

Cat lovers respect them for their stand-offishness. Seemingly, it is a price worth paying for their unique personalities.

Dogs are loyal, intelligent (according to their owners) and biddable – ever willing to please. For them, the owner is a much loved parent who must be obeyed and pleased.

Dogs put their own happiness second. There are many truly amazing stories of dogs' unswerving loyalty. The city of Edinburgh honours Robbie, a terrier who kept vigil over his master's grave for years. A cat would have too much respect for itself, and its own comfort, to do this.

A happy dog will learn tricks for his/her master. Its tail wags on seeing him/her.

Imagine asking a cat for its paw? The cat will look at you in amusement and pity. It is not being stupid; it merely wants to know why you (an allegedly intelligent human) would want to play such a silly game?

Dog owners appreciate the close bond they develop with their pets. Cat owners must be content to pamper and serve their beauties.

They are breeds apart – the owners, that is.

Comprehending   I

Question A

1.   What qualities do you admire most/least in cats?

2.   Do you think that this article backs up the view that a dog is man's best friend? Give reasons for your answer.

3.   Is this a fair and balanced article? Or is there a preference expressed for one type of pet?

Question B

Write a short article for a young persons' magazine (primary school children) on the subject of keeping pets. You must give advice and offer useful suggestions.

∽ TEXT 2 ∾

This article by Grace Wynne-Jones appeared in the Irish Times. *It examines the idea of bringing pets into the office.*

SUPER FURRY ANIMALS

Some of us are getting used to a new type of colleague who tends to wander around or sleep for hours, curled up somewhere cosy. He also keeps an eye out for snacks and likes to go for a walk at lunchtime. And before you decide that he sounds like Seán from the post room, it should be pointed out that this colleague says woof and remains blissfully above office politics.

His job is to cheer up his human companions, reduce their stress and perhaps even boost their productivity.

"People are taking themselves far too seriously," says Peter Fitzpatrick, a Dublin estate agent who brings his dog Prine to the office. "A dog really lightens up the workplace."

Even Philip Treacy, the milliner, has learned the value of having a dog on the premises. He calls his Jack Russell, Mr Big, his best friend and says he "provides light relief when we are all working. Fashion can be such a serious business, you need someone clowning around."

Despite such enthusiastic converts, Ireland is lagging behind in the workplace-pets phenomenon. Many Americans bring Fido or even Felix to the office, and some UK workers are lobbying to have parrots and hamsters in addition to more conventional relaxants, such as tanks of tropical fish.

A survey of 1,500 workers and employers in Britain found that 56 per cent of respondents thought that having pets in the office would boost the atmosphere and increase productivity. Their hunch seems backed up by American research, where 73 per cent of companies that allow pets past reception claim that it makes for a more productive workplace; 27 per cent said it had led to less absenteeism.

Comprehending

Question A

1. From reading this article, what are the advantages of having a pet in the workplace? Support your answer with reference to the text.
2. Do you think that this is a well-researched and well-written article? Give reasons for your answer.
3. What disadvantages, in your opinion, are there with regard to bringing pets into a workplace? Explain your answer.

Question B

Write a short report that an employee might write to his/her employer on the topic of pets in the workplace.

ഇ TEXT 3 ഇ

TRIGGS

In this article from 'An Irishman's Diary' column in the Irish Times, *Frank McNally writes about footballer Roy Keane and his faithful friend, Triggs.*

Roy and his female Labrador, Triggs, have been inseparable in times of crisis. Whenever the TV crews descended on the Keane mansion, they could rely on the spectacle of the footballer emerging for his daily walk, with the dog desperately trying to keep up. Roy would be bristling with energy and aggression. Triggs would be bristling with nothing, except bristles. Labradors use up all their energy being good-natured. If there were any barking to be done at the media, Roy always had to do it himself.

Keane once said he trusted Triggs more than he trusted his Man Utd team-mates, which admittedly was faint praise. But now that he can no longer lambaste fellow players and even managers for their low standards, how long will it be until his relationship with Triggs comes under strain? How long before Roy turns his ferocious gaze on his former best friend and bitterly rebukes her for accepting the mediocrity of being a Golden Labrador? For the moment, at least, the partnership continues to undermine the theory that dogs and their owners come to resemble each other eventually.

It's hard to decide which canine breed would best mirror Keane's looks and personality. The greyhound has many of Roy's qualities. Lean and hungry, it spends its professional career chasing a goal that always recedes before it. The hound may notch up countless victories but never catches the electric hare and remains frustrated. On the other hand, only a pit-bull terrier could match Keane's aggression, whether towards opponents or colleagues. If you were picking a dog to match Roy Keane's intelligence it would have to be the Alsatian.

Comprehending I

Question A

1.   What evidence is there that Roy Keane is a dog lover?
2.   According to this article, what qualities does Roy Keane possess?
3.   Do you like or dislike this article? Give reasons for your answer.

Question B

"If you were picking a dog to match Roy Keane's intelligence, it would have to be an Alsatian."

You have been asked to write a short humorous article for a magazine. Your assignment is to write about five famous people, using an animal to represent each. What animal would you chose for each person? Explain your reasons.

COMPOSING

1.   Write an account of the importance of pets in your life.

2.   Write a humorous story in which a pet tells his life story.

3.   Write a diary describing an interesting week in an animal's life.

4.   Write an article for a young people's magazine on the subject of celebrities. In this article, you must say what animal each celebrity resembles and why.

5.   Write a speech addressed to your class on the motion, "Cruelty to animals must be punished with long jail sentences."

6.   'My favourite animal' – write your views on this topic.

7.   Write a story in which an animal plays an important part.